HEART-LED LEADERSHIP

Inspiring the Workforce of Tomorrow

JUSTIN N. CHASE

For more information, email justin@jncstrategicsolutions.com.

ISBN: 979-8-89694-679-3 - Ebook
ISBN: 979-8-89694-680-9 - Paperback
ISBN: 979-8-89694-762-2 - Hardcover
ISBN: 979-8-89694-763-9 - Audiobook

To my beloved wife and our three wonderful children, your unwavering support and encouragement have been my guiding light throughout this journey. Every late night and early morning spent writing was made easier by your understanding and love. Thank you for your patience, for believing in me, and for filling our home with inspiration. I am eternally grateful to you all.

Table of Contents

Introduction

In today's rapidly evolving workplace, leadership is being redefined. As Millennials and Generation Z become the predominant force in the workplace, their expectations, values, and aspirations are reshaping professional environments. Unlike previous generations, they seek more than just a paycheck; they desire purpose, connection, and a sense of belonging. To meet these evolving expectations, leaders must move beyond traditional models and embrace a more human-centered approach. This book explores how leading with heart can inspire and engage the next generation of employees, creating workplaces that foster trust, innovation, and well-being.

I am a leader, mentor, and advocate for a fresh approach to leadership. Throughout my career, I have observed the transformation of workplace culture, driven by the evolving expectations of younger generations. Traditional leadership models have often prioritized results over relationships, but today's workforce demands a more human-centered approach—a heart-led leadership style. This style fosters open communication, encourages innovation, cultivates empathy, builds trust, and promotes emotional intelligence. Most importantly, it creates a culture where employees feel psychologically safe and empowered to contribute their best work.

By embracing heart-led leadership, I have helped my organizations cultivate environments where employees feel valued and motivated. This book reflects my journey and insights, offering practical guidance for leaders who seek to adapt and thrive in a new era of leadership.

This book explores the core principles of heart-led leadership, including authenticity, purpose, inclusivity, and well-being, and examines the broader shifts transforming today's workforce, from changing values to the impact of technology and the post-pandemic work environment. Finally, it offers actionable strategies to help leaders integrate these principles into their organizations, fostering long-term success and sustained employee engagement.

Whether you are a seasoned leader, a manager, or an aspiring professional, this book will help you navigate the complexities of the modern workforce. It offers a clear roadmap for cultivating a workplace culture that resonates with the values of today's employees. Through real-world examples and practical insights, you will learn how to build trust, empower your team, and create a sense of purpose that drives both individual fulfillment and organizational success.

Today's emerging workforce is the most diverse, socially conscious, and technologically savvy generation in history. Their expectations around work-life balance, corporate responsibility, and personal growth challenge traditional leadership norms. Organizations that fail to adapt risk losing top talent and falling behind in an increasingly competitive landscape. By embracing heart-led leadership, you can future-proof your leadership style and create a workplace where employees are engaged, fulfilled, and motivated to excel.

Understanding the New Workforce Landscape

To lead effectively in today's rapidly evolving world, we must first pause to understand the profound shifts shaping the modern workforce. We are no longer guiding teams molded by the industrial era's predictability or the optimism of the dot-com boom. Instead, we are leading a new generation—Millennials and Generation Z—who have come of age amid continuous technological disruption, global crises, and evolving societal norms.

Younger generations bring with them a different set of expectations. They have witnessed institutions falter and reform, observed the power of collective action through social movements, and developed a healthy skepticism toward authority that lacks authenticity and purpose. For them, work is more than a paycheck; it is a platform for impact. They are not simply asking, "What do I get from this job?" but rather, "What does this job say about who I am, and how does it contribute to the world?"

They seek meaning in their work, often choosing roles that align with their values over those that offer financial gain alone. The traditional nine-to-five schedule holds little appeal unless it is balanced with flexibility, autonomy, and a clear respect for their well-being. They want to learn, grow, and contribute to organizations that not only speak about change but actively pursue it, from embracing sustainable practices to building inclusive cultures.

Technology has played an integral role in shaping this reality. Having grown up in a digitally connected world, these employees expect seamless communication and intuitive collaboration tools. Yet beyond the devices and platforms, they crave something deeper: a sense of belonging and a human connection in an increasingly high-tech environment.

The Pandemic's Lasting Influence

The COVID-19 pandemic did more than disrupt daily routines; it rewrote the playbook for what work could and should look like. Practically overnight, remote work became the norm, prompting a widespread reevaluation of priorities. Many people, especially younger professionals, discovered they were more productive and happier with flexible schedules. They began to question long commutes, rigid hierarchies, and outdated policies that prioritized output over well-being.

Mental health moved to the forefront, not as a perk but as a priority. Workers began asking for empathy from managers, who were reminded that behind every screen was a human being navigating a complex life. As a result, organizations were compelled to reimagine leadership, not as command and control but as support and empowerment.

The Heart of the Matter: What It Means to Lead with Heart

In response to this cultural shift, a new leadership paradigm has emerged, one rooted in empathy, authenticity, and purpose. Heart-led leadership is not a soft alternative to traditional leadership models; it is a powerful, people-centered approach that fosters both well-being and measurable results.

At the heart of this model is emotional intelligence, the capacity to understand and manage one's own emotions while attuning to the emotions of others. Leaders with high emotional intelligence are fully present, listen deeply, and communicate with transparency.

They also recognize the importance of psychological safety and, to that end, create environments where employees feel seen and heard. In such workplaces, individuals are encouraged to share ideas, challenge the status quo, and take calculated risks without fear of retribution. Mistakes are viewed as learning opportunities, not failures.

Authenticity is another cornerstone of heart-led leadership. Gone are the days when leaders wore masks of perfection. Today's workforce values vulnerability and trusts leaders who admit when they don't have all the answers, share personal stories, and lead from a place of integrity.

Heart-led leaders also connect individual contributions to a larger organizational purpose. They do more than set goals; they help their teams understand why those goals matter. When people believe their work is meaningful, they show up differently. They care more, contribute more, and stay longer.

Moving From Theory to Practice

Embracing heart-led leadership is not merely about adopting a new mindset—it's about putting that mindset into consistent practice. It involves fostering open dialogue, giving and receiving feedback with humility, and consistently appreciating the people who keep the organization moving forward.

Heart-led leadership means leading by example—not only through words but through actions. When you demonstrate resilience during uncertainty or show compassion in moments of conflict, you model the behavior you wish to see. And when you extend genuine trust, offering both autonomy and accountability, you empower your team to realize their full potential.

Heart-led leadership also involves investing in your team's growth, not only through formal training but through mentorship, coaching, and opportunities to stretch into new roles. And along the way, you celebrate not just the big wins but also the quiet, often unseen moments of progress.

Why Heart-Led Leadership Works

Step into an organization or team led by a heart-led leader, and you can sense a difference almost instantly. Teams led with heart tend to be more engaged, more innovative, and more loyal. They aren't merely performing; they are thriving. Turnover decreases, creativity flourishes, and the organization establishes a reputation as a place where people do not just work, they belong.

Customers and clients notice, too. In a world increasingly hungry for trust and transparency, companies that lead with heart earn reputations that attract top talent and inspire lasting brand loyalty.

Looking Ahead

Leadership is no longer about climbing the ladder; it's about building bridges: between people, values, and vision. As we look ahead, one thing is certain: heart-led leadership isn't just a trend; it's the way forward.

In the chapters ahead, we will explore each principle of heart-led leadership in greater depth. You will encounter real stories, gain practical tools, and be invited to reflect on your own leadership journey.

Together, we have the opportunity to redefine what leadership looks like in the twenty-first century—and to build workplaces where people no longer have to choose between success and humanity.

Chapter 1

The Business Cost of Disengagement

"Highly engaged employees make the customer
experience; disengaged employees break it."

– Timothy R. Clark

Generation Z (born roughly between 1997 and 2012) and Millennials (born between 1981 and 1996) now make up the majority of today's workforce. However, recent studies indicate that both cohorts report lower levels of employee engagement compared to older generations. Disengagement, when employees do only the bare minimum without offering discretionary effort, has become an increasing concern for organizations.

According to Gallup (2023), 54 percent of Generation Z employees and 48 percent of Millennials are not engaged at work, rates worse than those of Gen X and Baby Boomers. This disengagement is often linked to "quiet quitting," in which employees disengage emotionally but remain physically present. Given that Millennials and Generation Z will make up approximately 58 percent of the workforce in 2025 (Deloitte, 2022), their level of engagement will have profound implications for organizations.

While many leaders focus on boosting engagement through policy changes or incentives, lasting engagement stems from leadership that connects with employees on a deeper level, an approach known as heart-led leadership. A heart-led leader leads with authenticity, empathy, and purpose, creating an environment where employees feel valued, heard, and inspired to contribute beyond their core responsibilities.

To fully understand the cost of disengagement and the transformative potential of heart-led leadership, we must examine its cascading impact across core business areas: performance, retention, innovation, and culture.

Impact on Business Performance and Productivity

One of the most immediate and measurable consequences of disengagement is a decline in productivity and performance. Disengaged employees lack motivation, leading to decreased efficiency, missed deadlines, and increased errors. According to Gallup (2023), global employee disengagement costs organizations approximately $8.8 trillion annually in lost productivity, equivalent to 9 percent of global GDP.

Millennials and Generation Z employees not only work more slowly when disengaged, but they also contribute to lower customer satisfaction. According to LumApps (2022), businesses with disengaged teams received customer ratings that were 10 percent lower than those with engaged teams. A case study in the retail sector revealed a 15 percent drop in sales at stores where employee disengagement was prevalent (Harvard Business Review, 2021).

Conversely, businesses that embrace heart-led leadership enjoy the opposite effect. When leaders foster genuine connection, employees are more likely to take ownership of their work. A culture rooted in trust and purpose transforms routine tasks into meaningful contributions, leading to increased productivity and better outcomes.

Turnover and Employee Retention Challenges

Beyond performance, disengagement significantly affects retention. Employees who feel disconnected are more likely to seek opportunities elsewhere. According to McKinsey & Company (2022), disengaged employees are 2.6 times more likely to look for a new job than their engaged counterparts. Deloitte (2022) reports that 40 percent of Generation Z workers and 35 percent of Millennials expect to leave their jobs within two years, and many are willing to do so even without another offer in hand.

The cost of turnover is substantial. Replacing an employee can amount to as much as one-third of their annual salary (Society for Human Resource Management, 2022), and each departure can trigger a ripple effect, destabilizing teams and amplifying dissatisfaction.

Heart-led leadership offers a powerful antidote to disengagement and turnover. When leaders invest in their people, building trust, supporting well-being, and showing authentic appreciation, they foster a sense of belonging. Employees who feel seen and empowered are more likely to stay and grow within the organization.

Effects on Innovation and Growth

Engagement is not only about output; it's also about imagination. Disengaged employees are significantly less likely to contribute creative solutions or take initiative. According to Harvard Business Review (2021), disengaged teams generate 60 percent fewer innovation suggestions than their engaged counterparts.

This loss of creativity is especially detrimental among Millennials and Generation Z, who offer fresh, tech-savvy perspectives in the workplace. When disengaged, they become hesitant to collaborate or share ideas. A case study in the tech sector revealed that a disengaged product development team doubled its time to market due to poor communication and a lack of ownership (MIT Sloan Management Review, 2022).

Heart-led leaders play a pivotal role in unlocking innovation. By cultivating psychological safety, they create spaces where employees feel confident in sharing bold ideas and challenging the status quo. Encouragement, not pressure, becomes the catalyst for breakthrough thinking.

Workplace Culture and Morale

The ripple effects of disengagement are felt in an organization's culture, shaping how teams interact and how morale is sustained. A toxic culture often results from disengagement going unchecked, manifesting in apathy, resistance, and breakdowns in collaboration. Eventually, this can create a divide between employees, damaging trust and team dynamics (Gallup, 2023).

Moreover, Millennials and Generation Z are especially sensitive to toxic environments and place a premium on purpose-driven work and an inclusive culture (Deloitte, 2022). When culture turns negative, it becomes a magnet for further disengagement and turnover.

Heart-led leadership can restore and elevate workplace culture. When leaders lead with empathy, integrity, and open communication, they shift the tone of the organization. Teams become more connected and motivated, not out of obligation, but because they see themselves as part of something greater.

Strategies for Business Leaders: Leading with Heart

In a time of growing generational disengagement, heart-led leadership is an absolute necessity. To re-engage Generation Z and Millennials, businesses should adopt leadership strategies that prioritize people over processes:

1. Authentic Leadership Practices
   - Foster trust and transparency in leadership communication.
   - Demonstrate genuine care for employees' well-being.
   - Lead with empathy and active listening.
2. Purpose-Driven Work Culture
   - Connect employees' daily tasks to a greater mission.
   - Encourage collaboration, creativity, and inclusivity.
   - Recognize and celebrate employee contributions beyond just metrics.

3. Growth and Development Opportunities
   - Provide meaningful mentorship and career development.
   - Allow employees to have a voice in decision-making.
   - Support work-life balance and mental health initiatives.

Disengagement among Millennials and Generation Z presents one of the most urgent challenges facing modern organizations. Yet within this challenge lies a powerful opportunity. By embracing heart-led leadership, companies can transform disengaged employees into inspired team members who bring their full energy and creativity to the workplace.

Ultimately, the future of work belongs to leaders who recognize that performance begins with people. Those who lead with heart—prioritizing authenticity, connection, and shared purpose—will not only elevate engagement but also shape organizations where people don't just work; they thrive.

As we've seen, disengagement among younger generations poses a serious threat to business outcomes, but it also offers a chance for organizations to reinvent how they lead. At the heart of every solution is the same truth: people long to be seen, heard, and valued. Heart-led leadership begins the transformation, but it is servant leadership that deepens it, shifting the focus from authority to service, from control to care. This next chapter begins with a timeless parable, *The Starfish Story*, which reminds us that even the smallest act of compassion can create a ripple of change. It challenges leaders to view individuals not as metrics, but as human beings with potential waiting to be empowered—one starfish at a time.

Chapter 2

The Starfish Story and Servant Leadership: Making a Difference One Step at a Time

Leading a business today often feels like navigating unpredictable tides, filled with constant demands, difficult choices, and unseen challenges beneath the surface. It's easy to become overwhelmed by the magnitude of it all, to wonder if individual efforts truly matter.

Yet, in these moments, the greatest leadership often emerges not from conquering the ocean, but from tending to a single starfish along the shore.

In this chapter, we explore servant leadership through the lens of *The Starfish Story*–a simple yet profound parable that emphasizes the importance of making a difference, no matter how small. By understanding this concept, business leaders can foster a culture of service, empathy, and growth within their organizations.

The Starfish Story

Early one morning, an old man went for a walk along the beach following a vicious storm. As he walked, he noticed a figure in the distance. As he drew closer, he saw a young boy pick something up from the beach and throw it into the sea. The boy then walked a few more steps and picked up something else and threw it into the sea. The old man was puzzled and concerned that the boy was up to no good. As he approached the boy, he asked, "What are you doing?" Without even looking up, the boy replied, "Throwing starfish back into the sea." The old man responded curiously, "why would you do that?" The boy quickly responded, "the tide is going out and soon it will be too hot, and the starfish will all die."

The old man chuckled, "the beach goes on for miles and there are thousands of starfish. Clearly you will never save enough to make a difference!" Again, the boy bent down, gently picked up a starfish and threw it into the sea. As it splashed down, the little boy turned to the man and said, "I made a difference to that one."

- Adapted from "The Star Thrower" by Loren Eiseley

The starfish story is a powerful parable that resonates deeply with the principles of servant leadership. This simple yet poignant narrative encapsulates a powerful lesson about individual agency and the importance of small actions in the face of overwhelming odds. The story serves as a metaphor for the struggles many face in life, where the enormity of problems can lead to feelings of helplessness. Yet, the child's determination to save even one starfish reflects a commitment to making a difference, no matter how small.

Servant Leadership: Defining the Concept

When Robert K. Greenleaf introduced the philosophy of servant leadership in the 1970s, he proposed a radical reimagining of what it means to lead. Rather than seeking power or prestige, the servant leader begins with a desire to serve, putting the needs, growth, and well-being of others before personal ambition. In doing so, they cultivate stronger, more human-centered organizations where people thrive. In an age where trust is currency and connection drives performance, servant leadership has moved from a fringe ideal to a vital framework for modern leadership.

Contrary to popular belief, servant leadership is not about relinquishing influence; it's about using that influence for the benefit of others. The servant leader is the nonprofit executive who quietly mentors young professionals to step into leadership roles. It's the school superintendent who meets with student groups to understand their lived experiences and lets their feedback shape district priorities. It's the healthcare administrator who makes time to walk the halls, not to audit, but to check in on staff and patients with genuine care.

One of the defining characteristics of servant leadership is **empathy**. Consider Rosalind Brewer, CEO of Walgreens Boots Alliance. Known for her people-first approach, Brewer made empathy a cornerstone of her leadership, and this was particularly evident during the COVID-19 pandemic. She prioritized the safety and well-being of employees across thousands of pharmacy locations, actively listening to their needs and ensuring support systems were in place, from mental health resources to hazard pay, while navigating public health responsibilities.

Another pillar of servant leadership is **listening**, truly hearing team members without pretense or interruption. Darren Walker, President of the Ford Foundation, is often credited with transforming the organization's culture through deep listening. He initiated wide-scale conversations with grantees and staff to understand their frustrations and hopes, then used those insights to restructure outdated systems. His example shows that when leaders pause to hear others, trust and transformation follow.

Servant leaders also foster **healing**, both individually and collectively. Following the death of George Floyd, companies around the world responded with statements, but few matched the intentionality of Merck's CEO at the time, Ken Frazier. As one of the few Black CEOs in the Fortune 500, Frazier used his platform to speak honestly about systemic injustice. Within Merck, he supported healing by hosting open forums and listening sessions for employees to process and share their emotions. This was leadership that prioritized humanity above headlines.

Awareness is another essential trait. Servant leaders are attuned to themselves, their teams, and the larger environment. Dr. Lisa Su, CEO of AMD, is known for her exceptional awareness of both market dynamics and team dynamics. Under her leadership, AMD transformed from near bankruptcy to becoming a leader in the semiconductor industry. Her ability to read the landscape while staying attuned to internal culture allowed her to align strategy with empathy, performance with purpose.

Rather than commanding compliance, servant leaders use **persuasion** to align people around a shared vision. Kip Tindell, co-founder of The Container Store, exemplified this approach. Instead of leading with rigid policies, he fostered open dialogue, inspiring employees through shared values and genuine enthusiasm. His ability to engage hearts and minds—not just job descriptions—resulted in remarkably low turnover and high employee satisfaction.

Conceptualization and **foresight** give servant leaders the capacity to think beyond daily operations and into the future. Whitney Wolfe Herd, founder and CEO of Bumble, exemplifies this mindset. From the beginning, she envisioned a company that would flip gender dynamics in online dating and create a safer, more empowering digital space for women. Her conceptual clarity, combined with foresight into shifting societal norms, helped her create a brand that was both disruptive and mission-driven.

Stewardship is about responsible leadership, caring for people and resources as if they were entrusted, not owned. At REI, the outdoor apparel company, stewardship is a living value. Its former CEO, Jerry Stritzke, made headlines when he closed all REI stores on Black Friday, encouraging employees and customers alike to spend time outdoors instead of shopping. That decision reflected a broader commitment to people, purpose, and the planet, a philosophy embedded in the company's cooperative structure and community-focused initiatives.

No servant leader is complete without a **commitment to the growth of others**. Melanie Perkins, CEO and co-founder of Canva, is known for cultivating a culture of growth from the ground up. Rather than focusing solely on rapid scaling, she has invested heavily in employee development, mentorship, and workplace equity. Her leadership has helped create a company where people feel both stretched and supported—an environment where growth is expected, but burnout is not.

And finally, servant leaders strive to **build community**. They see workplaces not just as engines of productivity but as ecosystems of belonging. Hamdi Ulukaya, founder of Chobani, has long made community a core priority. He hired refugees, shared company profits with employees, and invested in local initiatives that elevated entire towns. His leadership style didn't just grow a yogurt brand; it grew a movement rooted in dignity and collective success.

Servant leadership is not a checklist. It is a way of being, a daily commitment to lift others, lead with integrity, and leave things better than you found them. In a world hungry for leaders who are real, responsible, and relational, the servant leader stands not above others but beside them, proving that influence rooted in service is the most powerful kind of all.

Servant leadership offers a powerful alternative to traditional top-down leadership models, inviting leaders to rethink their purpose and approach. By centering leadership on service rather than authority, this model cultivates trust, engagement, and a sense of shared purpose within teams and organizations. It recognizes that sustainable success stems not from control but from empowering others to grow and thrive. As workplaces continue to evolve, the principles of servant leadership offer a timeless and human-centered framework, one that not only elevates individuals but also strengthens the collective, guiding organizations toward more ethical, compassionate, and resilient futures.

The Intersection of the Starfish Story and Servant Leadership

The spirit behind servant leadership aligns naturally with the deeper meaning of the *Starfish Story*: that individual actions, grounded in empathy and purpose, can create extraordinary ripple effects. Servant leaders don't need sweeping power to make change; they need the courage to act with intention, one person at a time.

We see this in business leaders like Cheryl Bachelder, former CEO of Popeyes Louisiana Kitchen, who transformed a struggling brand not by commanding from the top but by humbly listening to those on the front lines. She met with franchisees across the country, asking how the company could better support them. Her commitment to empowering others led not only to improved morale but to a surge in growth and profitability. Bachelder exemplifies a core principle of servant leadership: valuing individual impact. When leaders believe in the potential of each person and invest in their growth, the results compound far beyond the initial effort.

Empathy is another cornerstone. Servant leaders show up for others not to fix or control but to understand. Arne Sorenson, the late CEO of Marriott International, was known for his genuine care for employees. During moments of crisis, he communicated openly and compassionately, reminding his team that people came before profits. His vulnerability and clarity became a source of strength for thousands. That kind of presence—tuning in, listening deeply, and responding with humanity—fosters trust and inspires loyalty.

In both servant leadership and the *Starfish Story*, there's an undeniable theme of persistence despite overwhelming odds. When leaders encounter seemingly insurmountable challenges, they stay grounded in their purpose. Consider Dr. Mona Hanna-Attisha, the pediatrician who exposed the Flint water crisis. Though not a business leader, her servant-hearted approach, advocating relentlessly for children and families despite backlash, demonstrated the power of moral courage. She didn't aim to fix everything at once. She focused on who was in front of her and what she could do right then. That is servant leadership in action.

Building community is another defining trait of servant leadership. Leaders like Leah Lizarondo, founder of 412 Food Rescue, have reimagined what collective impact can look like by mobilizing thousands of volunteers to deliver surplus food directly to people in need. Her approach creates connection, not only between people and meals but between individuals and purpose. Servant leadership thrives in this type of collaborative, inclusive environment. It isn't about hierarchy or status; it's about shared ownership, mutual support, and lifting each other up.

These leaders also lead with foresight, recognizing that sustainable, meaningful change rarely happens overnight. It begins with small, intentional decisions repeated over time. In the healthcare industry, for example, organizations like Cleveland Clinic have strategically prioritized employee well-being, recognizing that long-term care for caregivers leads to better outcomes for patients and stronger institutional health. That investment in people, even when not immediately measurable, reflects the servant leader's long view.

Servant leadership doesn't require dramatic gestures. It requires a shift in posture—a willingness to lead from beside rather than above. It's about seeing people, hearing them, and empowering them to thrive. Like in the *Starfish Story*, the impact of those quiet, consistent acts may not be visible from afar. But up close, to the person whose life is touched, it means everything.

In this way, the ethos of servant leadership is not just compatible with the *Starfish Story*; it brings it to life, one human interaction at a time.

The *Starfish Story* and servant leadership together offer a compelling reminder that meaningful change often begins with small, intentional acts of service. In a world that frequently prioritizes scale and speed, these principles re-center our attention on the power of individual impact, empathy, and long-term growth. Servant leaders, like the child in the story, challenge the status quo not by trying to save everyone at once but by showing up consistently for the one in front of them. By embodying this mindset, leaders cultivate a culture of care, resilience, and purpose, proving that when we lead with heart, every effort truly does matter.

Practical Applications of the Starfish Story in Servant Leadership

To effectively integrate the lessons from the starfish story into servant leadership practices, leaders can adopt several strategies:

1. Cultivate a Culture of Empathy

Servant leaders prioritize the needs of their team members, and foster an environment where open communication and mutual respect thrive. By actively listening and demonstrating genuine concern for the well-being of their staff, these leaders create a sense of belonging that empowers individuals to share their thoughts and feelings. This empathetic approach not only strengthens relationships within the team, but also enhances collaboration, innovation, and overall morale. This ultimately leads to a more engaged and productive workforce.

In practice, servant leaders take the time to understand the perspectives, emotions, and challenges of their team members. This can be facilitated through regular one-on-one meetings, team discussions, or informal check-ins, where leaders encourage open communication and create safe spaces for sharing. By demonstrating that they value and respect their employees' feelings, servant leaders foster a deeper connection and trust within the team. This practice not only helps individuals feel heard but also cultivates a sense of belonging, which is essential for a thriving organizational culture.

2. Recognize Individual Contributions

In a servant leadership framework, leaders actively acknowledge the unique skills, talents, and efforts of each individual within the team. This recognition fosters a culture of appreciation and respect, where employees feel valued and motivated to perform at their best. By highlighting individual achievements, servant leaders not only boost morale but also empower team members to take ownership of their roles, enhancing overall team cohesion and productivity.

Servant leaders can create platforms for peer recognition, encouraging team members to acknowledge one another's contributions. This can be accomplished through collaborative tools, such as recognition boards, intranet sites, team meetings dedicated to sharing successes, where individuals can express gratitude for their colleagues' efforts. By fostering an environment where recognition is a shared practice, servant leaders empower employees to celebrate each other, cultivating a supportive and cohesive team atmosphere. This not only enhances individual motivation but also strengthens team dynamics, as members feel valued and appreciated, ultimately driving higher engagement and productivity throughout the organization.

3. Provide Opportunities for Development

By supporting the developmental needs of their team members, servant leaders recognize that their development contributes not only to personal fulfillment, but also to the overall success of the organization. By investing in training, mentorship, and skill-building initiatives, these leaders empower their employees to enhance their capabilities and pursue their career aspirations. This commitment to professional growth not only builds trust and loyalty within the team but also cultivates a culture of continuous learning and innovation.

Another effective application is the implementation of continuous learning initiatives, such as workshops, training sessions, and online courses. Servant leaders can learn the developmental needs of their teams and provide access to relevant resources that enhance both technical and soft skills. By investing in professional development opportunities, such as leadership training, conflict resolution, or communication skills workshops, leaders demonstrate their commitment to the growth of their team members. Encouraging employees to share what they have learned with their peers fosters a culture of knowledge sharing and collaboration. This approach not only empowers individuals to take charge of their own development, but also strengthens the organization as a whole by creating a more skilled and adaptable workforce.

4. Foster Collaboration

One key aspect of servant leadership is fostering collaboration through inclusive decision-making. Servant leaders intentionally involve team members in discussions about project direction and organizational strategy, ensuring that diverse perspectives are considered. By creating forums for open dialogue–such as team meetings, brainstorming sessions, or feedback platforms–they encourage participation and collective problem-solving. This not only harnesses the unique insights of each team member but also strengthens commitment to the outcomes, as individuals feel a sense of ownership over the decisions made.

Another important dimension of collaboration is the establishment of mentorship and peer-support programs. Recognizing the value of learning from one another, servant leaders facilitate opportunities for team members to collaborate on skill development and knowledge sharing. By pairing experienced employees with newer ones or encouraging cross-functional teamwork, they create an environment where collaboration becomes a vehicle for growth. This approach enhances individual capabilities while also nurturing a sense of community within the organization, reinforcing the idea that success is a collective endeavor. Through these collaborative practices, servant leaders cultivate a supportive and engaged workforce dedicated to mutual success.

5. Model Resilience

Servant leaders model resilience by maintaining a positive attitude and a steadfast commitment to overcoming obstacles, even in difficult situations. When leaders face setbacks, they openly communicate their thought processes and coping strategies, showcasing how to adapt and learn from adversity. This transparency not only inspires team members to cultivate their own resilience but also encourages a culture where challenges are viewed as opportunities for growth rather than insurmountable barriers.

To further nurture resilience within their teams, leaders can promote a supportive environment that prioritizes the well-being and mental health of their team. They can implement practices such as regular check-ins, wellness programs, and stress management resources to help employees navigate pressures effectively. By encouraging open discussions about resilience and coping mechanisms, servant leaders create a safe space for team members to share their experiences and seek support. This proactive approach not only strengthens individual resilience but also builds a cohesive team dynamic where members feel empowered to face challenges together, enhancing overall organizational resilience.

6. Lead by Example

Servant leaders lead by example, setting the tone for the values and behaviors expected within an organization such as work ethic, integrity, and commitment. For instance, when leaders prioritize transparency in their decision-making processes and openly communicate challenges and successes, they create an environment of trust and accountability. This openness encourages team members to adopt similar practices, fostering a culture where honesty and collaboration are valued. By actively taking part in team projects and showing a willingness to engage in tasks alongside their employees, leaders can illustrate the importance of teamwork and dedication.

Servant leaders can model empathy and respect in their interactions by demonstrating how to treat others with kindness and understanding. For example, when leaders take the time to listen to team members' concerns and provide support during difficult times, they show that caring for one another matters to the organization. This behavior not only sets a powerful example but also encourages employees to extend the same empathy to their colleagues and clients. By acknowledging their own mistakes and sharing lessons learned, servant leaders promote a growth mindset that values continuous improvement. This practice enhances individual development while also cultivating a supportive atmosphere where team members feel safe to take risks and learn from their experiences.

7. Feedback Mechanisms

Establishing robust feedback mechanisms ensures that employees feel heard and valued. One way of doing this is by implementing regular one-on-one check-ins between leaders and team members. These meetings provide an opportunity for employees to discuss their progress, share challenges, and receive constructive feedback tailored to their specific needs. By creating a safe space for honest dialogue, servant leaders can actively listen to their team members, address concerns, and provide guidance. This personalized approach not only enhances individual performance but also reinforces the leader's commitment to their growth, ensuring that feedback serves as a valuable tool for development rather than criticism.

Servant leaders can establish anonymous feedback channels, such as surveys or suggestion boxes, to encourage honest input from team members. These tools can be useful for gathering insights into team dynamics, leadership effectiveness, and organizational processes without the fear of repercussions. By actively seeking and using this feedback, servant leaders demonstrate their willingness to learn and adapt based on the needs of their team. Sharing the outcomes of the feedback collected and the actions taken in response fosters a sense of ownership among employees, highlighting the importance of their voices in shaping the work environment. This transparent approach not only strengthens trust but also cultivates a collaborative culture where continuous feedback is embraced as a pathway to mutual growth and success.

8. Community Engagement

By actively taking part in local initiatives and fostering partnerships with community organizations, servant leaders can make quick local connections. For instance, they might organize volunteer days where team members can join together to support local charities or environmental projects. By encouraging employees to participate in these activities, servant leaders not only show a commitment to social responsibility but also provide opportunities for team bonding and personal growth. This engagement helps build a positive organizational reputation within the community and reinforces the idea that the organization is invested in the well-being of its surroundings, creating a sense of shared purpose among employees.

Servant leaders can facilitate community engagement by creating platforms for employees to share their skills and knowledge with locals. This could involve hosting workshops, offering mentorship programs, volunteer opportunities, or providing resources to local schools or nonprofits. By empowering team members to contribute their expertise, servant leaders foster a culture of service that extends beyond the workplace. They can encourage employees to identify, and support causes they are passionate about, aligning community efforts with individual interests. This approach not only enhances community ties but also nurtures employee satisfaction and engagement, as team members feel fulfilled by their contributions to the greater good.

The practical application of the starfish story within servant leadership demonstrates that meaningful leadership is rooted in consistent, intentional action, no matter how little the action may be. By fostering empathy, recognizing individual contributions, encouraging growth, and building a culture of collaboration, servant leaders bring the story's lessons to life, one person, one moment at a time. These strategies, while often small in scale, create a ripple effect that transforms teams and organizations from the inside out. Ultimately, servant leadership reminds us that true impact doesn't come from grand gestures alone, but from a steady commitment to serving others with purpose, compassion, and integrity; proving, like the child on the beach, that every act of care makes a difference.

Challenges of Servant Leadership

While servant leadership offers numerous benefits, it also presents challenges that leaders must navigate.

1. Balancing Authority and Service

Servant leaders strive to uphold their commitment to serving others while also maintaining the necessary authority to guide their teams effectively. Servant leaders prioritize the needs of their team members, often placing a strong emphasis on collaboration and support. This can lead to a potential dilution of authority, as employees may become accustomed to the more egalitarian approach, and begin to act in a manner that blurs the lines of responsibility and decision-making. When leaders are overly focused on serving and accommodating their team, they may struggle to enforce necessary boundaries or make tough decisions, which can lead to confusion and inefficiencies within the organization.

2. Resistance to Change

Servant leaders strive to create a culture of growth and adaptability, but they may face some resistance to this new culture, which often stems from fear of the unknown, discomfort with new processes, or a perceived threat to job security, making it difficult for leaders to implement necessary changes effectively. Servant leaders, who prioritize the needs and concerns of their team, may find it particularly challenging to address these fears while also advocating for progress. This resistance can lead to frustration and disengagement, hindering the overall effectiveness of the team and causing delays in implementing new initiatives or strategies.

3. Measuring Success

Unlike conventional leadership styles, the success of servant leadership is not easily quantifiable. The servant leadership approach emphasizes qualitative outcomes such as employee satisfaction, team cohesion, and community impact rather than traditional quantitative metrics. This makes it difficult to apply conventional performance indicators that often overlook these aspects. For instance, while metrics such as sales figures or project completion rates may indicate success, they may not fully capture the emotional and relational dynamics within the team. This discrepancy can create challenges in demonstrating the effectiveness of servant leadership practices, leading to potential misunderstandings about what constitutes success in an organization that values service over strict performance metrics.

While servant leadership is rooted in noble intentions and transformative values, it is not without its complexities. Striking the right balance between serving and leading, navigating resistance to change, and redefining how success is measured require thoughtful strategy, self-awareness, and resilience. These challenges highlight that servant leadership is not a passive or simplistic model. Instead, it is a model that demands strength, clarity, and courage to lead with both heart and accountability. When embraced with intentionality, these tensions can become opportunities for deeper connections, meaningful growth, and more authentic leadership that aligns both people and purpose.

The starfish story reminds us that individual actions matter, and that empathy, growth, and community are essential to effective leadership in the new corporate environment. By embracing the lessons from the starfish story, leaders can create a culture that empowers individuals, fosters collaboration, and drives meaningful change.

As we reflect on the simplicity and depth of the starfish story, we are reminded that while authority and power are key aspects of leadership, serving others and making a difference, even if it's one person at a time, is just as important. In a world where challenges abound, let us embrace the spirit of servant leadership and commit to nurturing those around us, transforming lives, and creating a brighter future for all.

While the starfish story grounds us in the quiet, compassionate essence of servant leadership, there are moments in history that demand bold vision and courageous ambition. One such moment came when President

John F. Kennedy stood before the nation and challenged Americans to reach for the moon. His words were more than a call to space; they were a masterclass in inspirational leadership. As we turn the page, we move from the power of small, compassionate acts to the power of unifying, aspirational vision. Both forms of leadership are necessary. Together, they remind us that great leaders serve others not only through empathy and presence but also by daring to dream big, galvanize action, and believe in what's possible.

Chapter 3

Reach for the Stars: John F. Kennedy's Moon Speech

"We choose to go to the Moon in this decade and do the other things, not because they are easy but because they are hard; because that goal will serve to organize and measure the best of our energies and skills, because that challenge is one that we are willing to accept, one we are unwilling to postpone, and one we intend to win, and the others, too."

–John F. Kennedy

On September 12, 1962, President John F. Kennedy delivered a speech at Rice University that would resonate throughout history as one of the most inspiring calls to action in the realm of leadership. Kennedy's moon speech stands as a pivotal moment in American history, showcasing the profound importance of leadership in the shaping of ambitious national goals. At its core, the speech articulated a vision for space exploration that transcended mere scientific curiosity; it framed the Moon landing as a symbol of American perseverance, innovation, and determination. By boldly stating that the United States would land a man on the Moon and return him safely to Earth before the decade's end, Kennedy galvanized a nation and inspired a generation to believe in the power of collective effort and visionary thinking. This leadership moment was not just about the technical challenges of space travel, but also about fostering a sense of unity and purpose in the face of global competition, particularly during the Cold War.

Kennedy's leadership was characterized by his ability to communicate complex ideas in an accessible manner, a trait which served him well as he effectively rallied public support for an ambitious space program. By framing the mission as a necessity, rather than an option, Kennedy inspired both the government and the private sector to invest in research, development, and education, laying the groundwork for monumental advances in technology and science. His vision ignited a sense of national pride and urgency, prompting citizens to embrace the idea of exploration and innovation as essential components of American identity.

Kennedy's moon speech underscored the transformative power of leadership in mobilizing resources and fostering collaboration across diverse sectors. The Apollo program became a model of how visionary leadership could drive both technological advancements and social progress. By advocating for investment in education and engineering, Kennedy positioned the space race as a catalyst for economic growth and workforce development.

His call to action resonated beyond the confines of government, inspiring private enterprise and academia to contribute to a shared national goal. Ultimately, Kennedy's ability to articulate a clear, compelling vision for the future exemplified the critical role of leadership in motivating individuals and institutions to transcend their limitations and achieve greatness.

This chapter explores the profound leadership lessons embedded in Kennedy's speech, demonstrating how his insights can apply to modern leadership challenges.

The Power of Vision

At the heart of Kennedy's speech was a clear and compelling vision. He stated, *"We choose to go to the Moon."* This powerful declaration not only defined a specific goal but also created a sense of purpose that resonated across the nation. Effective leaders understand the importance of establishing a vision that is both ambitious and attainable. Such vision serves as a beacon, guiding the efforts of individuals and teams toward a common objective.

Kennedy's vision extended beyond mere space exploration; it symbolized American ingenuity, resilience, and determination. By articulating a bold vision, he instilled hope and excitement in the American public, fostering a collective identity rooted in ambition and progress. Modern leaders can learn from this approach by crafting a vision that is not only aspirational but also inclusive, inviting diverse stakeholders to join in the pursuit of shared goals.

Embracing Challenges

Kennedy did not shy away from acknowledging the challenges that lay ahead. He stated, *"This is not a task for a day, a year, or a decade."* His recognition of the complexities involved in achieving the Moon landing highlighted the reality that significant accomplishments require perseverance and resilience. Borrowing from his playbook, leaders must embrace challenges as inherent to the journey toward success.

By openly discussing the obstacles, Kennedy set realistic expectations while simultaneously motivating his audience to confront difficulties head-on. Being able to do this is a key trait of effective leaders, as it helps them foster a culture that encourages team members to view challenges as opportunities for growth and learning. This mindset prepares individuals to tackle adversity and also strengthens the organization's resolve in the face of setbacks.

Commitment to the Cause

Kennedy's unwavering commitment to the Moon mission was palpable. He proclaimed that the United States would land a man on the Moon and return him safely, by the end of the decade, a statement that conveyed both determination and urgency. This level of commitment is crucial for effective leadership. When leaders exhibit steadfast dedication to their vision, it inspires confidence among their followers.

Kennedy's commitment galvanized the nation, leading to increased funding for NASA and a surge of interest in science and technology. A leader's passion can be contagious; it motivates team members to invest emotionally in the mission. By demonstrating commitment, leaders can rally their teams, fostering a sense of ownership and accountability that drives collective effort.

The Importance of Teamwork

Kennedy emphasized the collective nature of the Moon landing when he said: *"We are all involved in this."* This acknowledgement of teamwork is a fundamental principle of effective leadership. No great achievement is accomplished in isolation; it requires collaboration among diverse individuals and groups.

Kennedy's recognition of teamwork highlighted the importance of building a supportive and inclusive environment. Leaders should encourage open communication and collaboration, ensuring that each team member feels valued and heard. By fostering a culture of teamwork, leaders can harness the strengths of their diverse teams, promoting creativity and innovation that leads to better outcomes.

Mastering Communication

Kennedy's speech was not just a presentation of facts; it was a masterclass in communication. He used evocative language and imagery to paint a vivid picture of the future, engaging his audience emotionally. Effective communication is a cornerstone of leadership, allowing leaders to convey their vision and inspire action.

Kennedy's ability to articulate complex ideas in accessible terms made his vision resonate with a wide audience. Modern leaders can learn from this by honing their communication skills, ensuring that their messages are clear, relatable, and impactful. Utilizing storytelling techniques can enhance engagement, allowing leaders to connect on a deeper level with their audiences.

Mobilizing Resources

Kennedy understood the necessity of mobilizing national resources to support the Moon mission. He called for substantial investment in space exploration, framing it as essential for national pride and technological advancement. Leaders must be adept at identifying and mobilizing the resources needed to achieve their goals.

This involves not only financial resources but also human talent and technological capabilities. Effective leaders are strategic in their resource allocation, ensuring that their teams have the tools and support they need to succeed. By advocating for the necessary resources and demonstrating their value, leaders can empower their teams to reach their full potential.

Fostering Innovation

"We shall send to the Moon, 240,000 miles away from the control station in Houston, a giant rocket more than 300 feet tall, the length of this football field, made of new metal alloys, some of which have not yet been invented, capable of standing heat and stresses several times more than have ever been experienced, fitted together with a precision better than the finest watch, carrying all the equipment needed for propulsion, guidance, control, communications, food and survival, on an untried mission, to an unknown celestial body, and then return it safely to earth, re-entering the atmosphere at speeds of over 25,000 miles per hour, causing heat about half that of the temperature of the Sun, and do all this, and do it right, and do it first before this decade is out—then we must be bold." – JFK Moon Speech, cont.

The Moon landing was not merely a goal; it represented a frontier of human knowledge and capability. Kennedy's vision encouraged a culture of innovation, urging scientists and engineers to push the boundaries of what was possible. Leaders must cultivate an environment that fosters creativity and experimentation.

Encouraging team members to take calculated risks and explore new ideas can lead to groundbreaking advancements. Kennedy's commitment to exploration serves as a reminder that great leadership involves embracing uncertainty and encouraging innovation. When leaders create a safe space for experimentation, they unlock the potential for transformative ideas and solutions.

Creating a Lasting Legacy

Kennedy framed the Moon landing as a legacy that would inspire future generations when he defined the mission as *"...a new frontier."* Leaders should consider the long-term impact of their actions and decisions, and strive to create a legacy that outlives them. A focus on legacy fosters a sense of purpose and responsibility, motivating leaders to make choices that align with their values and vision.

By prioritizing long-term goals and sustainability, leaders can inspire their teams to think beyond immediate challenges. A legacy-driven approach encourages individuals to consider the broader implications of their work, fostering a sense of pride and commitment to the mission.

Building Resilience and Adaptability

In the face of uncertainty, Kennedy's leadership exemplified resilience and adaptability. He acknowledged the unpredictability of the journey to the Moon, emphasizing that success would require flexibility and perseverance. Effective leaders must also cultivate resilience within themselves and their teams ahead of the inevitable challenges they would encounter—expected or not.

Kennedy's call to action was not merely about reaching a destination; it was about the journey of exploration and discovery. Leaders should encourage their teams to embrace change and adapt to evolving circumstances inherent in the process of attaining their goals. By fostering a culture of resilience, leaders can empower their teams to remain focused and motivated despite adversity.

Inspiring Future Generations

Kennedy's vision for space exploration was not just about the present; it was an investment in the future. He understood the importance of inspiring the next generation of leaders, scientists, and innovators. Effective leaders recognize their role in shaping the future and take deliberate actions to cultivate talent and inspire young minds.

By mentoring and supporting emerging leaders, seasoned leaders can create a ripple effect that extends far beyond their immediate impact. Encouraging youth engagement in STEM (Science, Technology, Engineering, and Mathematics) fields, for instance, aligns with Kennedy's vision of progress and exploration. Leaders should actively seek opportunities to inspire and empower the next generation, ensuring that their legacy continues.

Do Not Neglect the Non-Shiny Objects

"...and do the other things..."

Remember, at that time, Kennedy was President of the United States while the Cold War raged on. The Moon landing project needed to be done in addition to everything else the President and the Government were focused on. When organizations embark on innovative and exciting new projects, it is crucial to not lose sight of their core business operations and responsibilities. Neglecting these foundational aspects can worsen customer satisfaction, operational efficiency, and overall stability. Core business functions improve customer trust and loyalty, providing the revenue that supports new initiatives. If a company diverts too much focus and resources away from its primary offerings, it risks alienating its existing customer base, ultimately jeopardizing its long-term success. Maintaining a strong core ensures that a company remains competitive and resilient, even as it explores new avenues for growth.

Balancing innovation with core business responsibilities fosters a culture of sustainable growth. While pursuing innovative projects can invigorate a company's brand and attract new customers, a firm foundation allows for better risk management and resource allocation. By ensuring that core business areas remain robust, organizations can experiment with new ideas without the risk of destabilizing their existing operations. This synergy enhances overall performance, while also creating a platform for iterative innovation, where lessons learned from core operations can inform and improve new initiatives. Ultimately, a dual focus on both core business and innovative endeavors positions companies to thrive in an ever-evolving marketplace.

John F. Kennedy's moon speech serves as a timeless source of inspiration and guidance for leaders across various domains. By establishing a compelling vision, embracing challenges, demonstrating commitment, and fostering teamwork, modern leaders can draw valuable lessons from Kennedy's leadership style. His emphasis on effective communication, resource mobilization, innovation, resilience, and legacy-building remains relevant in today's complex and dynamic world.

As leaders reflect on Kennedy's words and actions, they are reminded of the profound impact that visionary leadership can have on individuals, organizations, and society as a whole. By embodying the principles demonstrated in Kennedy's moon speech, leaders can inspire their teams to reach for the stars, transforming ambitious dreams into tangible realities.

While Kennedy's moon speech exemplifies the power of bold, visionary leadership, it also underscores a deeper truth: great leadership is rooted in purpose. It is not enough to aim high—leaders must know *why* they lead and help others find meaning in the mission. This sense of purpose sustains momentum long after the initial excitement fades. In the next chapter, we turn to the insights of Stephen Covey, whose work on purpose-driven leadership provides a practical framework for aligning vision with values. Where Kennedy inspired a nation to reach the moon, Covey helps leaders stay grounded in principles that ensure each step toward the goal is intentional, ethical, and deeply meaningful.

Chapter 4

The Value of Purpose-Driven Leadership

"The main thing is to keep the main thing the main thing."

– Stephen Covey

In today's fast-paced and often chaotic business environment, the concept of purpose-driven leadership has emerged as a beacon of clarity and direction for organizations and individuals alike. At the heart of this leadership philosophy lies a powerful idea articulated by Stephen Covey's quote. This quote encapsulates the essence of purpose-driven leadership, emphasizing the importance of focusing on what matters most to drive organizational success and personal fulfillment.

As we delve into the value of purpose-driven leadership, we will explore its core principles, benefits, and practical applications while drawing on Covey's wisdom. This exploration will reveal how leaders who prioritize purpose can inspire their teams, foster resilience, and create a lasting impact.

Understanding Purpose-Driven Leadership

In an era marked by rapid change, global uncertainty, and rising employee expectations, purpose-driven leadership has emerged as a defining characteristic of the most effective and respected leaders. At its core, purpose-driven leadership is rooted in the belief that leadership is not just about managing people or processes, it's about aligning every action, decision, and goal with a deeper sense of meaning. Leaders who lead with purpose are guided by more than performance metrics or quarterly results; they are driven by a compelling "why" that anchors them, inspires others, and sustains momentum through both triumph and trial.

Purpose acts as a north star, steady and constant, helping leaders navigate the complexities and pressures of modern leadership. It becomes the lens through which strategy is shaped, culture is cultivated, and impact is measured. Organizations led by purpose-driven leaders tend to be more resilient, more innovative, and more cohesive because the people within them believe they are working toward something bigger than themselves.

Defining Purpose

Purpose is not as simple as a slogan on a wall or a neatly worded mission statement—it's what keeps an organization alive and kicking. It defines *why* the organization exists beyond profit making, and *what* contribution it aims to make to the world. Purpose energizes people. It offers clarity in chaos and motivation in moments of challenge.

Take Patagonia, for example, whose purpose, "We're in business to save our home planet," shapes every decision, from product design to activism. That clarity attracts employees and customers who share those values and are inspired to be part of a broader movement, not just a brand. In this way, a clearly articulated purpose becomes a rallying cry, uniting people across roles and regions to move in the same direction with conviction.

For leaders, defining and communicating this purpose is a foundational responsibility. When teams understand the *why*, their work becomes more of a contribution, than a job. Purpose gives people something to believe in. Belief fuels commitment, effort, and engagement.

The Role of Values

If purpose is the destination, values are the compass. Values shape culture, influence behavior, and serve as a moral guardrail for decision-making. They guide how people treat one another, how leaders lead, and how the organization shows up in the world. Purpose without values tends to be performative or hollow. But when deeply held values support a clear purpose, the result is authenticity of action, trust, and long-term alignment.

Purpose-driven leaders don't just talk about values, they embody them. Consider Rose Marcario, former CEO of Patagonia, who not only led with conviction but modeled the company's values by taking bold stances on environmental issues, even when it meant challenging the political or economic status quo. Her leadership sent a clear message: values are non-negotiable.

In practice, values help employees align their personal beliefs with the organization's mission. When this alignment exists, it fosters a deep sense of belonging and intrinsic motivation. People feel part of something bigger than themselves, not just as workers, but as human beings who share in the organization's identity and purpose. In such an environment, people do not merely comply, they commit.

Purpose-driven leadership creates organizations that are not only more profitable but more principled. It moves teams beyond the transactional and into the transformational. As we will explore in the next section, Stephen Covey's framework for principle-centered leadership builds on these ideas, showing leaders how to live their values daily, lead with intention, and cultivate trust as the cornerstone of high-performance culture.

The Importance of Keeping the Main Thing the Main Thing

Covey's words, "The main thing is to keep the main thing the main thing," serve as a reminder to focus on priorities that drive meaningful outcomes. In the context of purpose-driven leadership, this means consistently aligning actions with the organization's purpose and values.

Clarity Amidst Chaos

In an increasingly chaotic world, where distractions abound and priorities often shift, maintaining focus on core objectives allows individuals and organizations to navigate complexities with clarity and purpose. By identifying and prioritizing what truly matters–whether values or mission–individuals can align their efforts and resources toward meaningful outcomes, reducing the noise that leads to confusion and inefficiency.

When chaos reigns, the impulse to react to immediate demands can overshadow the bigger picture. Covey advocates proactive decision-making, which begins with a clear understanding of one's fundamental priorities. By consciously choosing to focus on the main thing, individuals can cultivate resilience and adaptability, allowing them to weather unexpected challenges without losing sight of their overarching goals. This clarity supports not only personal development but also enhances team dynamics, as shared objectives foster collaboration and a collective sense of purpose.

Keeping the main thing the main thing serves as a guiding principle for ethical leadership and accountability. In times of uncertainty, leaders who clearly articulate and uphold core values can inspire trust and commitment among their teams. This alignment not only streamlines decision-making but also ensures that actions taken are consistent with organizational values, fostering a culture of integrity and transparency. Ultimately, by adhering to Covey's principle, individuals and organizations can transform chaos into a structured path toward success, reinforcing the significance of clarity in both personal and collective endeavors.

Resilience in Adversity

Purpose-driven leadership inspires resilience. When challenges arise, leaders who anchor their decisions with a clear purpose can maintain their composure and guide their teams through adversity. This resilience is contagious; teams that understand their purpose are more likely to persevere during tough times, as they see their work as part of a greater mission.

Resilience in the face of adversity is about more than just enduring; it's about adapting and thriving despite challenges. When we focus on our primary goals, we develop a sense of direction that fuels our determination. This focus acts as an anchor during turbulent times, enabling us to make informed decisions that align with our values. Covey's teachings encourage us to prioritize tasks that reflect our long-term vision, rather than get sidetracked by immediate pressures or crises. While this approach enhances our problem-solving capabilities, it also fosters a mindset geared toward growth and perseverance.

Maintaining clarity about our priorities empowers us to leverage adversity as a catalyst for personal development. When faced with setbacks, those who embody Covey's principle are more likely to view challenges as learning opportunities rather than insurmountable obstacles. By keeping the main thing, the main thing, we cultivate a resilient mindset that propels past less than favorable circumstances. This resilience not only helps us overcome individual challenges but also inspires those around us, creating a culture of perseverance and commitment to shared goals. In essence, Covey's philosophy serves as a bedrock for navigating life's complexities with better focus.

Enhancing Decision Making

Keeping the main thing the main thing also enhances decision-making processes. Leaders who keep their organization's core purpose in sight tend to make informed choices that align with that purpose. This alignment ensures that decisions are strategically and ethically sound, reinforcing the integrity of the organization.

By prioritizing what truly matters, leaders can streamline their efforts, minimize distractions, and enhance clarity in their decision-making processes. This focus allows for more deliberate choices that align with long-term goals, rather than getting sidetracked by less significant issues or immediate pressures.

For instance, in a business context, leaders who keep the main thing in mind are more likely to allocate resources effectively, invest in initiatives that drive growth, and foster a culture of accountability. Ultimately, this alignment propels organizations forward and prevents them from being busy with irrelevant pursuits.

Prioritizing the main thing cultivates resilience in the face of challenges and distractions. In an ever-changing environment, individuals often encounter competing priorities that dilute their effectiveness. Covey's principle promotes a disciplined approach to decision-making, allowing leaders to navigate complexities with confidence. By consistently returning to their core mission, they can make choices that not only resolve immediate issues but also contribute to a sustainable path for success. *Keeping the main thing the main thing* is not just a mantra; it is an essential practice for enhancing decision-making and achieving meaningful outcomes.

The Benefits of Purpose-Driven Leadership

The value of purpose-driven leadership extends far beyond easily quantifiable organizational success; it has profound implications for employee engagement, innovation, and overall well-being.

Increased Employee Engagement

Employees are more engaged when they understand their role in achieving a larger purpose. Purpose-driven leaders create an environment where individuals feel connected to their work and are motivated to contribute to the success of the organization. Engaged employees are often more productive, creative, and committed to their organization's success. When leaders articulate a clear and compelling purpose, it is more likely to resonate with employees, allowing them to see their work as more than mere tasks and responsibilities. This sense of connection enhances job satisfaction and motivation, as employees feel that they are part of something larger than themselves. Engaged employees are more likely to exhibit higher levels of productivity, creativity, and commitment, driving the organization toward its goals.

Purpose-driven leadership cultivates a collaborative and inclusive workplace culture. When leaders prioritize purpose, they encourage open dialogue and participation in decision-making processes. This inclusivity not only empowers employees but also fosters a sense of belonging and community within the organization. Employees who feel valued and heard are more inclined to contribute their ideas and insights, and this can lead to innovative solutions and improvements. The resulting collaborative environment strengthens teamwork, resulting in a more agile and adaptive organization.

Finally, because employees under purpose-driven leaders are more engaged with an organization's mission and vision, they are more likely to remain with such an organization over a long time, even when they are presented with better offers. This stability is beneficial for organizations as it reduces the costs associated with hiring and training new employees. A workforce that is engaged and passionate about its mission is also more likely to represent the organization positively to external stakeholders, thereby enhancing its reputation and attracting top talent. Purpose-driven leadership not only inspires employees but also creates a sustainable competitive advantage.

Attracting and Retaining Talent

When organizations clearly articulate their purpose, they create a compelling narrative that resonates with potential employees. Individuals are increasingly seeking workplaces that align with their values and offer a sense of meaning in their daily tasks. By prioritizing purpose-driven leadership, companies not only enhance their recruitment efforts but also cultivate a strong employer brand that appeals to top talent. This alignment fosters a sense of belonging and ownership among employees, leading to increased job satisfaction and reduced turnover.

Purpose-driven organizations often experience enhanced performance and productivity. When employees feel connected to a higher purpose, they are more likely to be engaged in their work and committed to the organization's goals. This engagement fosters increased creativity, collaboration, and innovation, as team members are motivated to contribute to something greater than themselves. By attracting talent that is not only skilled but also aligned with the organization's mission, companies can build a dynamic workforce that drives exceptional results and maintains a competitive edge in their industry.

Retaining talent in a purpose-driven environment contributes to long-term organizational sustainability. Employees who are emotionally invested in their work are more likely to stay with the organization, reducing recruitment and training costs. A stable workforce enhances team cohesion and promotes knowledge sharing, which is vital for maintaining a learning culture. Purpose-driven leadership also fosters a positive organizational culture that attracts like-minded individuals, creating a virtuous cycle of engagement and retention. Ultimately, by prioritizing purpose, organizations can create a resilient workforce that is equipped to navigate challenges and seize opportunities in an ever-changing business landscape.

Fostering Innovation and Creativity

A clear purpose encourages innovation. By cultivating an environment where innovation thrives, purpose-driven leaders empower their employees to think outside the box, suggest new ideas and challenge existing norms. This enhances problem-solving capabilities while fostering a culture of collaboration and engagement, as team members feel valued and motivated to contribute their unique perspectives.

As emphasis on creativity allows organizations to adapt more swiftly to changing market dynamics and societal needs. In today's fast-paced world, the ability to pivot and innovate is crucial for sustainability and growth. Leaders who prioritize creativity encourage their teams to experiment and learn from failures, and this is vital for developing resilient strategies. Such adaptability not only positions organizations to respond effectively to external challenges but also enhances their capacity to seize new opportunities that align with their mission.

Nurturing innovation and creativity within a purpose-driven framework leads to greater employee satisfaction and retention. When team members are encouraged to express their creativity and contribute to meaningful projects, they experience a sense of fulfillment and purpose in their work. This connection to a greater mission fosters loyalty and reduces turnover, which is beneficial for both the organization and its employees. Ultimately, leaders who support innovation and creativity not only achieve business success but also cultivate a thriving workplace culture rooted in passion and commitment to the organization's purpose.

Building Stronger Relationships

Purpose-driven leadership fosters stronger relationships, both within the organization and with external stakeholders. When leaders prioritize relationships, they create an environment where team members feel valued and understood. In a purpose-driven context, where the focus is on shared values and goals, strong relationships help align individual aspirations with the organization's mission. This alignment enhances engagement and encourages collective commitment to achieving common objectives.

Strong relationships enable leaders to better understand the diverse perspectives and needs of their team members. By cultivating empathy and active listening, purpose-driven leaders can foster an inclusive atmosphere that inspires collective contribution. This inclusivity enhances creativity and problem-solving and strengthens the team's resilience. When challenges arise, a foundation of strong relationships allows for more effective collaboration and support, enabling the team to navigate obstacles together and emerge stronger.

The ability to build strong relationships can significantly enhance a leader's ability to inspire and motivate their team. When leaders authentically connect with their team members, they can more effectively communicate the organization's purpose and vision. This emotional connection helps ignite passion and commitment, transforming individual efforts into a collective drive toward achieving impactful results. Ultimately, the strength of relationships within a purpose-driven leadership framework can catalyze positive change, ensuring that the organization not only meets its goals but makes a meaningful and lasting impact on the community and beyond.

Practical Applications of Purpose-Driven Leadership

To fully realize the benefits of purpose-driven leadership, leaders must take intentional steps to embed purpose into their organizational culture and practices.

Articulating a Clear Purpose

Purpose-driven leadership is built on a clear purpose which serves as the guiding light for both leaders and their team members. When leaders effectively communicate their vision and objectives, they create a shared understanding that aligns individual efforts with organizational goals. This clarity helps to foster a sense of belonging and commitment among team members, as they see how their contributions fit into the larger picture. A well-defined purpose not only motivates employees but also encourages collaboration toward achieving a common goal.

In practical terms, purpose-driven leaders can articulate their purpose through consistent messaging and storytelling. By sharing personal anecdotes and real-life examples, they illustrate how the organization's mission impacts the lives of customers, employees, and the community. This storytelling approach not only makes the purpose more relatable but also reinforces its importance. Leaders should encourage open dialogues, inviting feedback and ideas from team members. This collaborative approach ensures that the purpose resonates at all levels of the organization and fosters a sense of ownership among employees.

Articulating a clear purpose involves integrating it into everyday operations and decision-making processes. Purpose-driven leaders must ensure that the organization's values are reflected in its policies, practices, and performance metrics. In doing so, they reinforce the idea that purpose is not just a lofty concept but rather a practical framework that guides the daily actions of the team. This alignment between purpose and practice enhances accountability and drives the organization toward its goals, ultimately leading to sustained success and a positive impact on stakeholders.

Integrating Purpose into Decision-Making

When leaders consciously incorporate purpose into their decision-making processes, they create a framework that guides choices and actions. This alignment not only enhances organizational coherence but also fosters a strong sense of belonging among employees. As team members begin to relate their work to a larger mission, their engagement and motivation increases, leading to improved performance and greater job satisfaction.

Purpose-driven decision-making encourages leaders to consider the broader impact of their choices on stakeholders, particularly the employees, customers, and the greater community. By evaluating decisions through the lens of purpose, leaders can prioritize initiatives that not only drive financial success, but also create positive social and environmental outcomes. For instance, a company committed to sustainability might choose to invest in eco-friendly technologies, even if it requires a higher initial cost. This approach not only supports the organization's values but also builds brand loyalty among customers who resonate with those principles.

Integrating purpose into decision-making nurtures a culture of accountability and transparency. When leaders clearly communicate the purpose behind their decisions, it cultivates trust and encourages open dialogue within the organization. Employees feel empowered to contribute ideas and feedback, knowing that their perspectives are valued in the context of the organization's mission. This collaborative environment enhances innovation and adaptability, positioning the organization to navigate challenges with resilience while staying true to its purpose. Ultimately, purpose-driven decision-making transforms the organizational landscape, leading to sustained success and a positive societal impact.

Modeling Purpose-Driven Behavior

By modeling the desired behavior, leaders can inspire their teams to engage actively with their work, fostering a culture where motivation stems from a shared vision rather than mere transactional goals. This alignment not only enhances job satisfaction but also promotes resilience during challenges, as employees feel connected to a cause greater than themselves. In practice, leaders can demonstrate this behavior by openly communicating their own purpose, encouraging team members to articulate their personal motivations, and ensuring that organizational objectives reflect these shared values.

Leaders can nurture purpose-driven behavior through various strategies. For instance, they can facilitate workshops that help employees identify their individual purpose and explore how these align with the organization's mission. By creating platforms for open dialogue, leaders can nurture a sense of community and belonging, where team members feel valued and empowered to contribute meaningfully. Additionally, recognizing and celebrating achievements that reflect the organization's purpose can reinforce this behavior, making it a tangible aspect of the workplace culture.

Ultimately, modeling purpose-driven behavior not only enhances individual and team performance but also drives organizational success. This approach leads to sustainable growth, as purpose-driven organizations tend to attract talent, retain employees, and build strong reputations in their industries. By prioritizing purpose in leadership, organizations can navigate complexities with agility and compassion, ensuring that their long-term strategies resonate with both their workforce and their wider communities.

Encouraging Employee Involvement

Engaging employees can foster a sense of ownership and commitment within the organization. When leaders articulate a clear and compelling purpose, employees are more likely to align their personal values with the organization's mission. This alignment not only enhances motivation but also encourages employees to actively take part in decision-making processes, contributing their unique insights and ideas. By creating an environment where employees feel valued and heard, organizations can tap into collective creativity and make innovative decisions, leading to more effective problem-solving and greater progress.

Purpose-driven leaders actively seek to cultivate a culture of collaboration and inclusivity. They understand that diverse perspectives enrich the organizational fabric and drive better outcomes. By encouraging teams to engage in open dialogues, share feedback, and work together toward common goals, leaders can break down silos and foster stronger relationships among employees. This collaborative spirit not only boosts morale but also reinforces a shared commitment to the organization's purpose, making it easier for teams to navigate challenges and celebrate successes together.

Recognizing and rewarding employee involvement plays a major role in reinforcing a more engaging organizational culture. Leaders should celebrate contributions of any size, and acknowledge the impact of collective efforts on achieving organizational goals. By implementing recognition programs and providing opportunities for professional growth and development, organizations can further motivate employees to take initiative and engage in meaningful work. Ultimately, when employees see that their involvement is valued and contributes to a larger purpose, they are more likely to become passionate advocates for the organization, driving its mission forward with enthusiasm and dedication.

Celebrating Successes Aligned with Purpose

Celebrating success is a vital expression of purpose-driven leadership, as it reinforces the shared sense of ownership that underpins purpose-driven organizations. When leaders take the time to recognize and celebrate achievements, they create a culture of appreciation that aligns with the organization's purpose. By publicly acknowledging individual and team successes, leaders highlight the behaviors and actions that exemplify the organization's purpose, thereby reinforcing its significance in everyday operations.

Celebrating success serves as a powerful motivator for improved engagement and productivity. Purpose-driven leadership emphasizes the importance of aligning personal and organizational values; when leaders celebrate achievements, they validate the hard work and dedication of their team members. This recognition not only uplifts spirits but also inspires individuals to strive for excellence in their roles, knowing that their contributions are valued and impact the larger mission. By consistently celebrating milestones, leaders can maintain momentum and enthusiasm, ensuring that the team remains focused on its shared purpose.

Celebrating success fosters a learning environment where reflection and growth are prioritized. Purpose-driven leaders recognize that every achievement is an opportunity to reinforce the lessons learned along the journey. By analyzing successes and celebrating the process, leaders encourage teams to adopt a mindset of continuous improvement. This practice not only deepens the team's commitment to the organization's purpose but also cultivates resilience and adaptability in the face of future challenges. In this way, celebrating success becomes an integral part of a purpose-driven leadership approach, enhancing both individual fulfillment and organizational effectiveness.

In summary, purpose-driven leadership is a powerful approach that emphasizes the importance of aligning actions with a clear and compelling purpose. Stephen Covey's quote, "The main thing is to keep the main thing the main thing," serves as a guiding principle for leaders seeking to navigate the complexities of modern organizational life.

By maintaining focus on what truly matters, purpose-driven leaders inspire their teams, foster resilience, and create lasting impact. As organizations continue to evolve in an ever-changing landscape, the value of purpose-driven leadership will remain a crucial element for success, enabling leaders to cultivate environments where individuals thrive and organizations flourish. Ultimately, it is the unwavering commitment to purpose that will distinguish exceptional leaders and organizations in the years ahead.

Yet even the most clearly defined purpose can be undermined without the character to uphold it. Purpose-driven leadership is not sustained by vision alone—it requires the humility to listen, to learn, and to lead with authenticity. In a world where authority is often mistaken for certainty, humility grounds leaders in self-awareness and strengthens their connection to others. As we turn to the next chapter, we explore why humility is not a weakness, but a quiet strength that elevates leadership from performative to transformational, allowing purpose to move from aspiration to lived experience.

Chapter 5

It's Not About You: Embracing the True Essence of Leadership

"Customers will never love a company until the employees love it first!"

– Simon Sinek

In the realm of leadership, a transformative shift is underway—one that redefines the very essence of what it means to lead. Traditionally, leadership has often been viewed through the lens of authority, charisma, and individual accolades, casting the leader as the hero in a narrative of success. Yet a deeper exploration reveals that true leadership transcends personal ambition and ego; it is fundamentally about the people being led. This chapter explores the idea that effective leadership is not a solitary pursuit but a collaborative journey where the collective strength and well-being of the team take precedence.

At the center of this perspective lies the recognition that the most impactful leaders are those who empower others. They cultivate an environment where individuals feel valued, heard, and motivated to contribute their best selves. By prioritizing the needs, aspirations, and growth of their team members, leaders can foster a culture of trust and collaboration. This chapter will delve into the principles of servant leadership, emotional intelligence, and the importance of active listening, illustrating how these qualities enable leaders to unlock their team's potential and drive collective success.

This chapter will also highlight real-world examples of leaders who have exemplified this people-centric approach, showcasing how their efforts have not only enhanced team performance but also created lasting legacies. By shifting the focus from the leader's individual achievements to the collective accomplishments of the team, we can cultivate a more inclusive and effective leadership model that resonates with today's increasingly diverse and interconnected world. Emphasizing community, shared goals, and mutual respect, this chapter aims to inspire current and aspiring leaders to embrace a more holistic view of their role in shaping the future.

The Foundation of Selflessness

At the heart of effective leadership lies selflessness, the quality of putting the needs and well-being of others before one's own interests or desires. It embodies a spirit of generosity and compassion, where individuals prioritize the welfare of their community, family, or colleagues over personal gain. This altruistic mindset fosters stronger relationships and builds trust, as selfless acts often lead to a sense of belonging and mutual support. Selflessness not only enhances personal fulfillment but also contributes to a more harmonious and interconnected society, where collective well-being is valued and nurtured.

Leaders who prioritize their own ambitions, accolades, or authority risk alienating their teams and hindering growth. In contrast, selfless leadership is characterized by a focus on the collective well-being of the group rather than individual glory. This approach creates an environment where team members feel valued and understood, fostering trust and collaboration.

One exemplary model of selfless leadership is Mahatma Gandhi, whose commitment to nonviolent resistance and social justice profoundly transformed India's struggle for independence. Rather than seeking personal power or accolades, Gandhi devoted his life to advocating for the rights of the oppressed, emphasizing the importance of community over individual ambition. He led numerous campaigns that prioritized the needs of the people, whether it was addressing poverty, promoting education, or fighting against discrimination. His ability to inspire and unite diverse groups around a common cause exemplifies how selfless leadership can effect meaningful change, demonstrating true influence lies not in authority but in the ability to uplift and empower others.

Another compelling example of selfless leadership is Dr. Paul Farmer, co-founder of Partners in Health, who dedicated his life to providing healthcare to impoverished communities around the world. Farmer's unwavering commitment to serving the most marginalized populations exemplified true selflessness. He worked tirelessly in Haiti, Rwanda, and other underserved regions to address health disparities and improve access to quality medical care. He often lived in the communities he served, prioritizing the needs of patients over his own comforts and safety. Through his innovative approaches to healthcare delivery and his advocacy for social justice, Farmer not only transformed lives but also inspired countless others to follow his lead, demonstrating that selfless leadership can create profound and lasting change in the world.

The Role of Humility

Humility is a vital attribute for any leader aiming to foster a culture of selflessness. Humble leaders are approachable, open to feedback, and willing to admit their limitations. They understand that they do not have all the answers and are eager to learn from their team. This humility invites team members to share their insights, creating a rich tapestry of ideas that can lead to innovative solutions.

For example, a humble leader might regularly solicit feedback from their team on project progress, demonstrating that they value the perspectives of those they lead. This practice not only enhances decision-making but also reinforces a culture where everyone feels inspired to contribute.

A prime example of humble leadership is Bill George, former CEO of Medtronic and a prominent advocate for authentic leadership. Known for his down-to-earth approach, George consistently emphasized the importance of serving others and prioritizing the needs of his team and stakeholders over his own ego. Despite his success, he remains approachable and values feedback from employees, believing that true leadership is about listening and learning. He often shares credit for achievements with his team, highlighting their contributions rather than seeking personal accolades. Through his humility and commitment to ethical leadership, George has inspired countless leaders to adopt a more servant-oriented approach, demonstrating that genuine humility can drive both personal and organizational success.

Active Listening: The Heart of Selflessness

Active listening is another critical aspect of selfless leadership. In a world filled with distractions, taking the time to truly listen to team members can be transformative. Active listening involves fully engaging with the speaker, acknowledging their feelings, and responding thoughtfully. When leaders practice listening, they foster a sense of belonging among team members, making them feel valued and understood.

Consider a scenario in which a team member is struggling with a project. A leader who actively listens will not only hear the words but will also sense the underlying emotions, showing empathy and providing the necessary support. This creates a culture where individuals feel safe to express their concerns and challenges, leading to greater collaboration and problem-solving.

Empathy

Empathy goes hand in hand with active listening. A leader who empathizes with their team can connect on a deeper level, acknowledging their challenges and their emotions. This connection fosters loyalty and motivates team members to work toward common goals. For instance, when a leader acknowledges the stress of a deadline and offers support or resources, it strengthens the bond within the team and reinforces a culture of care.

A notable example of selfless leadership is Nelson Mandela, whose life and legacy exemplify the principles of sacrifice and service to others.

After enduring 27 years in prison for his fight against apartheid, Mandela emerged not seeking revenge or personal gain, but rather promoting reconciliation and healing in a deeply divided South Africa. He prioritized the welfare of his nation over his own desires, advocating for peace and equality while encouraging both sides to come together. By fostering dialogue and understanding, Mandela not only helped dismantle systemic racism, but also inspired a generation to pursue justice with empathy and compassion. This way, he demonstrated that true leadership is rooted in selflessness and a commitment to the greater good.

Empowering Others

Empowerment is another crucial aspect of selfless leadership which emphasizes that it's not just about the leader. When leaders empower their team members, they create an environment where individuals can take ownership of their work, make decisions, and contribute meaningfully to the organization. This not only enhances individual morale but also drives collective success.

A notable example of a leader empowering their team is Indra Nooyi, the former CEO of PepsiCo, who championed a culture of inclusivity and collaboration throughout the organization. Nooyi actively sought input from employees at all levels, encouraging them to voice their ideas and contribute to the company's strategic direction. She implemented programs that focused on personal development and mentorship, empowering team members to take initiative and pursue their career aspirations. By emphasizing the importance of diverse perspectives and fostering a supportive environment, she not only inspired innovation within PepsiCo but also cultivated a sense of ownership among her employees, demonstrating how a leader can elevate their team and drive collective success through empowerment.

The Power of Delegation

Effective delegation is a hallmark of empowering leadership. By distributing responsibilities and trusting team members with important tasks, leaders demonstrate their confidence in their team's abilities. This delegation not only alleviates the leader's burden but also fosters a sense of accountability and pride among team members.

Delegation allows leaders to focus on strategic initiatives rather than getting bogged down in micromanagement. It encourages team members to develop their skills and take initiative, ultimately resulting in a more dynamic and innovative team. Leaders who recognize that their role is to guide and support, rather than controlling, empower their teams to think creatively and solve problems independently.

Fostering a Growth Mindset

Empowering leaders also cultivate a growth mindset within their teams. A growth mindset emphasizes the belief that abilities can be developed through dedication and hard work. Leaders can encourage this mindset by providing opportunities for learning and development, recognizing team members' efforts, and celebrating their progress. This can take many forms, including mentorship, training programs, and opportunities for cross-functional collaboration. Leaders who invest in their team's professional development send a clear message: the success of the team is more important than the leader's personal accolades.

For example, a leader who encourages team members to pursue their interests and develop new skills demonstrates a commitment to their growth. This not only enhances individual capabilities but also builds a stronger, more versatile team. When team members feel that their development is a priority, they are more likely to remain engaged and motivated.

Creating a Shared Vision

A compelling vision is essential for effective leadership, but it should not stem solely from the leader. Instead, it should be a collaborative effort that includes input from all team members. When leaders involve their teams in the vision-setting process, they cultivate a sense of ownership and commitment to the collective goals.

A notable example of a leader creating a shared vision is Oprah Winfrey, who built her brand and media empire around the idea of empowerment and personal growth. From the outset, Winfrey articulated a vision of emotional connection and self-improvement, encouraging her audience and her team to embrace their potential and pursue their passions. Through her talk show and various platforms, she fostered a sense of community, by inviting viewers and employees to share their stories and aspirations. By aligning her team around this vision of empowerment and authenticity, Winfrey not only inspired them to contribute creatively but also cultivated a culture where everyone felt invested in the mission of making a positive impact on people's lives. Her ability to articulate this vision has been instrumental in her success, demonstrating how a leader can unite and motivate a diverse group toward a common goal.

Collaborative Vision Setting

Collaborative visioning sessions provide an opportunity for team members to contribute their perspectives and ideas. These sessions can take various forms, such as brainstorming workshops, focus groups, or informal discussions. By facilitating open dialogue, leaders can gather valuable insights that enrich the vision and ensure it resonates with everyone.

During these sessions, leaders should actively encourage participation, making it clear that all ideas are welcome. This inclusive approach not only strengthens the vision but also fosters a sense of ownership among team members. When individuals feel that their voices matter, they are more likely to rally behind the vision and work collaboratively toward its realization.

When team members feel that they have a stake in the vision, they are more likely to be motivated to achieve it. They become ambassadors for the vision, spreading enthusiasm and commitment throughout the organization. This shared sense of purpose transforms the team's dynamic, shifting the focus from the leader's authority to the collective ambition of the group.

Aligning Values and Goals

Aligning the team's values and goals with the broader organizational mission is another critical aspect of collaborative visioning. Leaders should facilitate discussions that help team members understand how their individual contributions align with the organization's objectives. This alignment reinforces the idea that the team's success is a collective effort rather than a reflection of the leader's influence.

When team members see the connection between their work and the organization's mission, they are more likely to feel a sense of purpose and commitment. This intrinsic motivation is far more powerful than external recognition, as it fosters a culture of dedication and resilience.

Leading by Example: The Power of Modeling Behavior

While leadership is not about the leader, it is essential for leaders to model the behavior they wish to see in their teams, as this reinforces the values of the organization and sets the tone for team dynamics. When leaders embody selflessness, empathy, and commitment to the collective, they inspire their teams to do the same.

Patagonia's founder, Yvon Chouinard, is known for his firm commitment to environmental sustainability and ethical business practices. Chouinard has consistently demonstrated his values in both his personal and professional life. He initiated practices such as using recycled materials in products and advocating for fair labor conditions, setting a standard for corporate responsibility in the outdoor apparel industry.

By personally engaging in environmental activism and encouraging his employees to do the same, Chouinard fosters a workplace culture that prioritizes social and environmental impact. His leadership not only inspires his team but also resonates with customers, proving that leading by example can drive both business success and positive change.

Demonstrating Vulnerability and Openness

One powerful way to lead by example is through vulnerability. Leaders who are willing to share their challenges, mistakes, and learning experiences create an environment where team members feel safe to take risks and learn from their failures. This openness fosters a culture of trust and collaboration, where individuals are encouraged to support one another.

When a leader admits to a misstep and discusses the lessons learned, it normalizes the process of growth and development. Team members are more likely to embrace challenges and innovate when they see that their leader values learning over perfection.

Celebrating Team Success

Another important aspect of leading by example is celebrating team success rather than seeking personal recognition. Leaders should publicly acknowledge the contributions of their team members and highlight the collective effort that led to success. This approach reinforces the idea that achievements result from collaboration, not individual prowess.

Celebrating team success can take many forms, from team shout-outs in meetings to more formal recognition programs. When leaders celebrate the team, they foster a sense of belonging and camaraderie, reinforcing the belief that everyone's contributions matter.

Navigating Challenges Together

Leadership is often tested during challenging times. How a leader responds to adversity can significantly affect their team's morale and resilience. In such moments, it becomes even more crucial to remember that leadership is not about personal glory but about navigating challenges as a united front.

A striking example of a leader navigating challenging times alongside his team is Brian Chesky, cofounder and CEO of Airbnb. During the onset of the COVID-19 pandemic, as travel came to a near halt and the company faced significant financial losses, Chesky took decisive action while maintaining open communication with his employees. He personally addressed the team through transparent updates, acknowledging the difficulties and uncertainties they faced. Rather than making unilateral decisions, he involved his team in discussions about the company's future and encouraged innovative thinking to adapt to the new landscape.

Chesky's empathetic leadership included difficult choices, such as significant workforce reduction, but he ensured that those affected were treated with dignity, respect and offered support. By fostering a sense of solidarity and collaboration during such turbulent times, Chesky not only steered Airbnb through the crisis but also strengthened the bonds within his team, emphasizing resilience and shared purpose in overcoming adversity.

Open and Transparent Communication

During difficult times, open communication is essential. Leaders must be transparent about the challenges the team faces and encourage dialogue about potential solutions. This approach not only builds trust but also empowers team members to contribute their insights and ideas.

When leaders create a safe space for discussion, they foster a culture of problem-solving and innovation. Team members are more likely to share their perspectives and collaborate on solutions when they feel that their voices matter.

Prioritizing Team Well-Being

In times of stress, leaders should prioritize the well-being of their team members. This may involve providing resources for stress management, encouraging work-life balance, or simply being available to listen. By demonstrating care and support, leaders reinforce the idea that the team's well-being is paramount.

When team members feel supported, they are likely to rally together against challenges, share burdens, and find creative solutions, ultimately emerging stronger as a unit.

Building a Legacy of Service

As leaders focus on the needs of their teams, they begin to build a legacy of service. This legacy is characterized by commitment to the growth and success of others, creating a ripple effect that extends beyond the immediate team.

A prominent example of building a legacy of service is Blake Mycoskie, founder of TOMS Shoes. Mycoskie pioneered the "One for One" model, where for every pair of shoes sold, a pair is donated to a child in need. This innovative approach not only addressed the immediate needs of underserved communities but also inspired a broader movement within the business sector to integrate social responsibility into their models. By prioritizing service and community impact alongside profitability, Mycoskie encouraged other businesses to adopt similar practices, proving that a commitment to social good can coexist with commercial success. His efforts have transformed the lives of countless children and established TOMS as a leader in the social enterprise space, leaving a lasting legacy that emphasizes the importance of giving back and making a difference in the world.

Mentorship and Support

One way to build a legacy of service is through mentorship. Leaders who invest time in mentoring their team members help shape the next generation of leaders. By sharing their knowledge, experiences, and insights, they empower others to grow and succeed.

Mentorship can take various forms, from formal programs to informal relationships. Regardless of the format, the goal is to support others in the pursuit of their goals. Leaders who mentor others not only contribute to their success but also reinforce the idea that leadership is about uplifting others.

Creating a Culture of Giving Back

Another aspect of building a legacy of service is fostering a culture of giving back. Leaders can encourage their teams to engage in community service, volunteerism, or social responsibility initiatives. This not only enhances the team's sense of purpose but also reinforces the idea that leadership extends beyond the workplace.

When team members take part in service initiatives, they develop a deeper understanding of the impact they can have on their communities. This sense of purpose can be incredibly motivating, creating a culture where individuals are inspired to contribute positively to the world around them.

The Dangers of Self-Centered Leadership

While the focus of this chapter has been on selflessness, it is important to acknowledge the dangers of self-centered leadership. Leaders who prioritize their own interests above those of their team or organization often create a toxic work environment. Their self-serving attitudes can erode trust among team members who may feel undervalued and overlooked. When leaders prioritize their personal goals, they may disregard the input and well-being of their employees, resulting in disengagement and low morale. A culture of fear and resentment can arise, stifling creativity and innovation as team members become hesitant to share their ideas or take risks.

Self-centered leaders tend to foster a competitive atmosphere rather than a collaborative one. When a leader's primary concern is their own success, they may pit employees against one another, encouraging unhealthy competition instead of teamwork. This can lead to divisions within teams, where individuals are more focused on their own achievements rather than working collectively toward a common goal. The lack of collaboration can stunt the growth of the organization as a whole, as shared knowledge and skills are not used effectively. In the long run, this can hinder the organization's ability to adapt to challenges and capitalize on opportunities, ultimately affecting its overall success.

Finally, the repercussions of self-centered leadership extend beyond the immediate team or organization to impact stakeholders and the broader community. Leaders who are not attuned to the needs and concerns of their employees often overlook the importance of corporate social responsibility and ethical practices. This can damage the organization's reputation, as stakeholders may perceive the company as exploitative or untrustworthy. Negative public perception can lead to a decline in customer loyalty and brand integrity, affecting profitability and long-term sustainability. In contrast, leaders who prioritize the collective well-being of their teams and stakeholders foster a more positive and productive organizational environment, contributing to overall success and growth.

The Impact of Ego

Ego-driven leadership often undermines collaboration and innovation. When leaders prioritize their image or status over the success of their team, they stifle creativity and hinder growth. Team members may feel discouraged from sharing their ideas or taking risks, fearing that they will be overshadowed or dismissed.

Self-centered leaders may struggle to build trust within their teams. When individuals perceive their leader as self-serving, they are less likely to engage openly, leading to a breakdown in communication and collaboration. This can create a vicious cycle, where disengagement and low morale further exacerbate the leader's need for control and recognition.

Recognizing the Signs of Self-Centered Leadership

It is crucial for leaders to recognize the signs of self-centered leadership within themselves. Self-awareness is the first step toward adopting a more collaborative and empowering leadership style. Leaders should regularly reflect on their motivations, seeking feedback from trusted colleagues and team members.

Signs of self-centered leadership may include an unwillingness to delegate, a tendency to take credit for the team's accomplishments, or a lack of interest in team members' personal and professional growth. By acknowledging these behaviors, leaders can take proactive steps to shift their focus from themselves to the needs of their team.

Embracing the True Essence of Leadership

Effective leadership is fundamentally about serving others rather than seeking personal recognition or authority. By embracing selflessness, empowering team members, fostering collaboration, and leading by example, leaders can create a culture in which everyone thrives.

As we navigate the complexities of leadership, let us remember that the most impactful leaders are those who prioritize their team's success over their own ambitions. Accolades matter less in leadership than the lives one touches, and the legacy of empowerment and collaboration one leaves behind. Ultimately, it's not about you; it's about the collective journey toward a shared vision, where every team member plays a vital role in achieving success together.

In a world that often glorifies the individual, true leadership stands out as a beacon of selflessness and service. By adopting this mindset, leaders can inspire others, drive innovation, and create a lasting impact on their organizations and communities. As we move forward, let us challenge the notion that leadership is about the leader and instead embrace the powerful belief that it is about the people we serve.

This people-first mindset naturally leads us to one of the most vital dimensions of leadership: genuinely caring for those one leads. Few embody this principle better than Richard Branson, whose philosophy centers on the belief that if you take care of your employees, they will take care of your business. In the next chapter, we will explore how placing employee well-being at the heart of leadership not only fosters loyalty and engagement but also fuels long-term organizational success. Through Branson's example, we will see how compassion, trust, and a commitment to people can transform workplace culture and elevate the impact of any leader.

Chapter 6

Take Care of Your Employees: Leadership Principles from Richard Branson

"If you take care of your employees, they will take care of the clients."

–Richard Branson

Effective leadership transcends mere management; it involves nurturing a culture where employees feel valued and empowered. Richard Branson, the founder of the Virgin Group, exemplifies this philosophy through his unwavering commitment to employee well-being. He famously believes that taking care of employees is paramount because they, in turn, will take care of the customers and drive the organization's success. This chapter delves into the critical importance of prioritizing employee care as a foundational leadership principle, illustrating how it can lead to enhanced productivity, employee loyalty, and a vibrant organizational culture.

Branson's approach emphasizes the idea that happy employees are the bedrock of any thriving company. By fostering an environment where employees feel respected and appreciated, leaders can unlock their potential and creativity. This chapter explores Branson's strategies, such as promoting open communication and providing opportunities for personal and professional growth. By putting employees first, leaders not only boost morale but also cultivate a sense of belonging, which is essential in today's competitive landscape. The impact of such a culture can lead to lower turnover rates and higher employee engagement, ultimately benefiting the organization as a whole.

In a world where dynamics of work are continually evolving, the principles championed by Branson serve as a guiding light for modern leaders. This chapter highlights real-world examples that demonstrate the tangible benefits of prioritizing employee care. As we navigate the complexities of leadership, it becomes increasingly clear that a genuine investment in people is not just a moral imperative; it is a strategic advantage that can propel organizations to new heights. By embracing this philosophy, leaders can create a more resilient and innovative workforce ready to meet the challenges of the future.

Who is Richard Branson?

Richard Branson is a renowned entrepreneur known for his innovative spirit and adventurous leadership style. Born in 1950 in London, Branson began his entrepreneurial journey at a young age, launching his first business, *Student* magazine, at sixteen. He achieved significant success with Virgin Records in the 1970s, establishing a diverse empire that includes airlines, telecommunications, and space exploration. Branson's ability to identify opportunities and challenge conventional norms has been a hallmark of his career.

Branson's leadership approach is characterized by a strong emphasis on creativity and employee empowerment. He believes that treating employees as the most valuable asset leads to higher morale and loyalty, fostering a collaborative and supportive work environment. His willingness to take risks and learn from failures has also defined his leadership; although many of his ventures have faced challenges, his resilience continues to inspire others to pursue their entrepreneurial dreams without fear of setbacks.

In addition to his business acumen, Richard Branson is deeply committed to social responsibility and sustainability. He actively advocates for various global issues, including climate change and education, through initiatives like the Virgin Unite foundation. By aligning his business goals with positive social impact, Branson exemplifies how successful entrepreneurship can contribute to the greater good. His visionary thinking, charismatic communication, and dedication to innovation continue to establish him as a significant figure in the business world and an inspiration to aspiring leaders.

The Value of Employee Care

Employee Engagement and Retention

Employee engagement is a critical driver of organizational success. Employees who feel valued and supported are more productive, more committed, and less likely to leave the company. By investing in employee care; through competitive salaries, comprehensive benefits, and a supportive work environment, companies can enhance retention rates. Such investment not only reduces costs associated with turnover but also builds a stable and experienced workforce.

Enhanced Productivity

Creating a work environment that prioritizes employee well-being is essential for fostering productivity. When employees are content and feel supported, they are more motivated and focused on their tasks. This increase in productivity contributes to better business outcomes and higher profitability. Organizations that invest in the well-being of their employees often realize a return on that investment in the form of increased efficiency and output.

Positive Workplace Culture

A focus on employee care cultivates a positive workplace culture. Such cultures are characterized by collaboration, respect, and open communication. Companies that prioritize these values often attract top talent and enjoy improved teamwork and creativity. A positive workplace culture not only enhances employee satisfaction but also strengthens the company's reputation, making it an employer of choice in the industry.

Innovation and Creativity

When employees feel supported and valued, they are more likely to take risks and propose innovative ideas. A culture that encourages creativity allows employees to express themselves freely, leading to ideas that can propel the company forward. This environment of trust and support is crucial for fostering innovation. By prioritizing employee care, organizations can create a space where creativity thrives, leading to new products, services, and processes that drive the company's growth and success.

Richard Branson's Leadership Principles

Richard Branson's approach to leadership serves as an exemplary model for organizations aiming to prioritize employee care. His principles highlight the importance of valuing individuals within the corporate structure.

Putting People First

Branson has always emphasized the principle of people before profits. He famously stated, "If you take care of your employees, they will take care of your business." This principle underscores the idea that a company's success is a direct reflection of the well-being of its employees. Branson's companies, such as Virgin Atlantic, thrives because he prioritizes the needs and satisfaction of his employees. By fostering a culture in which employees are the priority, companies can create a loyal and committed workforce that drives business success.

Encouraging Autonomy

Branson believes in empowering employees to take ownership of their work. By granting them autonomy, he fosters an environment where employees feel trusted and valued. This empowerment leads to higher job satisfaction and encourages employees to take initiative, resulting in increased creativity and productivity. Autonomy allows employees to leverage their unique skills and perspectives, leading to innovative solutions and enhanced performance.

Promoting Work-Life Balance

Recognizing the importance of work-life balance, Branson has implemented flexible working arrangements within the Virgin Group. He understands that happy employees are those who can balance their professional and personal lives. This consideration not only enhances employee satisfaction but also leads to greater loyalty and commitment to the organization. By supporting work-life balance, companies can reduce burnout and improve overall well-being, creating a more sustainable and engaged workforce.

Creating a Fun Work Environment

Branson's leadership style incorporates elements of fun and enjoyment in the workplace. He advocates for a culture where employees can express their personalities and enjoy their work. This approach not only makes the workplace more enjoyable but also fosters creativity and collaboration among team members. A fun work environment encourages employees to connect with each other and the organization, leading to stronger team dynamics and improved morale.

Investing in Employee Development

Branson is a vigorous proponent of continuous learning and development. He believes that investing in employees' growth, through training, mentorship, and career development opportunities, creates a more skilled and motivated workforce. Organizations that prioritize employee development often see higher levels of engagement and satisfaction, contributing to overall success. By supporting career growth, companies can harness the full potential of their employees, leading to innovation and competitive advantage.

Case Studies: Virgin Group

To illustrate the effectiveness of Branson's leadership principles, we can look at various initiatives undertaken by the Virgin Group.

Virgin Atlantic and Employee Empowerment

Virgin Atlantic has set a standard for employee empowerment in the airline industry. Branson encouraged employees to break traditional hierarchies, enabling them to make decisions that enhance customer service. This empowerment led to higher employee satisfaction and contributed to Virgin Atlantic's reputation for exceptional service. By trusting employees to make decisions, Virgin Atlantic has created a culture of accountability and innovation.

Virgin Unite and Social Responsibility

Branson founded Virgin Unite, the non-profit foundation of the Virgin Group, to tackle social and environmental issues. This initiative not only reflects Branson's commitment to social responsibility but also engages employees by allowing them to contribute to meaningful causes. Employees feel more connected to their work when they see their organization making a positive impact on society. This sense of purpose enhances employee engagement and strengthens the company's brand.

Virgin Mobile

Another prime example is Virgin Mobile, where Branson created an environment that encourages creativity and innovation. Employees are given the freedom to experiment with new ideas, resulting in groundbreaking marketing campaigns that differentiate Virgin Mobile from its competitors.

Flexible Work Policies Across Virgin Companies

In various Virgin companies, Branson has implemented flexible work policies that allow employees to choose how and where they work. This flexibility has been beneficial during challenging times, such as the COVID-19 pandemic, demonstrating the value of adapting to employees' needs and preferences. Flexible work arrangements support work-life balance and enable employees to perform at their best, increasing satisfaction and productivity.

The Ripple Effect of Valuing Employees

When organizations prioritize employee care, the benefits extend beyond the immediate workforce.

Customer Satisfaction

Happy employees lead to happy customers. When employees are engaged and motivated, they provide better service, which enhances customer satisfaction and loyalty. This positive cycle can significantly boost a company's reputation and profitability. By creating a culture that values employees, companies can improve their customer experience and drive business success.

Attracting Top Talent

Companies known for valuing their employees are often more appealing to prospective job candidates. In an age of talent scarcity, organizations that prioritize employee well-being can attract and retain the best talent in their industry. A reputation for employee care can differentiate a company in the job market, making it a preferred employer for top talent.

Positive Brand Image

Organizations that take care of their employees often enjoy a positive brand image. This reputation can lead to increased customer loyalty, positive media coverage, and a stronger market position. Companies that are perceived as responsible by employers often benefit from enhanced customer trust and loyalty. A strong brand image built on employee care can drive long-term success and competitiveness.

Measuring Employee Engagement

To fully realize the benefits of employee engagement, organizations must measure and analyze engagement levels. Various tools and techniques can be employed, including surveys, feedback sessions, and performance metrics.

Key Metrics to Consider

1. Employee Satisfaction Surveys

Regularly conducting surveys to gauge employee sentiment can provide valuable insights into employees' perceptions of their work environment, job roles, and overall organizational culture. By gathering feedback on various aspects: such as communication, recognition, professional development opportunities, and work-life balance, these surveys help identify areas where employees feel connected and motivated, as well as those that may require improvement. Analyzing the responses allows organizations to gauge the level of engagement among their workforce, pinpoint specific issues that may hinder productivity or morale, and implement targeted strategies to enhance overall satisfaction. This proactive approach not only fosters a more engaged workforce but also contributes to higher retention rates and improved organizational performance.

2. Turnover Rates

Turnover rates serve as a critical indicator of employee engagement within an organization, as high turnover often signals underlying issues related to job satisfaction, workplace culture, or employee commitment. When employees leave frequently, it can suggest that they are not fully invested in their roles or that their needs and expectations are not being met. By analyzing turnover rates alongside exit interview data, organizations can identify patterns and specific reasons for departures, revealing insights into employee morale and engagement levels. A lower turnover rate typically reflects a more engaged workforce, where employees feel valued and connected to their work, while a high rate may prompt organizations to re-evaluate their engagement strategies and address any areas of concern to foster a more positive and committed work environment.

3. Productivity Metrics

Tracking productivity levels can indicate the effectiveness of engagement initiatives. Productivity metrics provide quantitative data on performance, output, and efficiency levels within an organization. By tracking metrics such as project completion rates, sales figures, and overall work quality, organizations can gauge how motivated and committed employees are to their tasks. High productivity often correlates with engaged employees who are invested in their work and driven to achieve organizational goals, while low productivity may indicate disengagement or a lack of motivation. Analyzing productivity trends over time can help identify the impact of changes in workplace culture, management practices, or employee support initiatives. This allows organizations to fine-tune their engagement strategies to enhance performance and foster a more collaborative and dynamic work environment.

4. Customer Satisfaction Scores

Engaged employees typically deliver better customer service. Customer satisfaction scores can serve as a valuable proxy for measuring employee engagement, as there is often a direct correlation between how engaged employees are and the level of service they provide to customers. Engaged employees tend to be more motivated, attentive, and committed to delivering high-quality experiences, which can lead to higher customer satisfaction ratings. By analyzing these scores, organizations can gain insights into the effectiveness of their workforce; consistent positive feedback from customers may indicate that employees are fully invested in their roles and take pride in their work. Conversely, declining customer satisfaction scores may signal disengagement among staff, highlighting the need for improved support, training, or recognition efforts. Ultimately, monitoring customer satisfaction in conjunction with employee engagement initiatives can help organizations create a more positive work environment that benefits both employees and customers.

Challenges and Solutions

While the benefits of taking care of employees are clear, organizations often face challenges in implementing these principles.

Resistance to Change

Some leaders may resist changing their traditional management styles. To overcome this, organizations can provide training and development for leaders, emphasizing the importance of employee care and the benefits it brings. By fostering a culture of continuous improvement, companies can encourage leaders to adopt fresh approaches that prioritize employee well-being.

Resource Constraints

Implementing employee care initiatives may require financial investment, which can pose a challenge for some companies. However, organizations can start small by introducing low-cost initiatives, such as flexible work schedules or employee recognition programs, and gradually expand their efforts. By demonstrating the value of these initiatives through measurable outcomes, companies can justify further investment in employee care.

Measuring Success

Organizations may struggle to measure the impact of employee care initiatives. Implementing employee feedback mechanisms, such as surveys and performance metrics, can help assess the effectiveness of these initiatives and guide future improvements. By leveraging data and feedback, companies can refine their strategies and ensure that employee care initiatives deliver the desired outcomes.

The value of taking care of employees cannot be overstated. Organizations that prioritize their workforce not only enhance employee satisfaction and retention but also drive productivity, innovation, and customer loyalty. Richard Branson's leadership principles serve as a powerful framework for understanding how to cultivate a culture of care within an organization. By putting people first, encouraging autonomy, promoting work-life balance, creating a fun work environment, and investing in employee development, leaders can foster a thriving workplace that benefits everyone involved. In an era where the employee experience is paramount, businesses must recognize that their greatest asset is their people, and investing in their well-being is the key to sustainable success. Through a commitment to employee care, organizations can achieve long-term growth, innovation, and competitive advantage.

While investing in employee well-being lays the foundation for a healthy, high-performing organization, the way leaders *show up* each day—through their tone, behavior, and attitude—can either reinforce or undermine that foundation. It's not enough to have the right policies or perks; leadership must be grounded in everyday decency, humility, and respect. Too often, ego, entitlement, or a lack of self-awareness erode trust and morale. In the next chapter, *Don't Be a D*ck*, we explore how simple human values—such as kindness, compassion, and the courage to lead with humility—are not only essential to effective leadership but are the very qualities that define it.

.

Chapter 7

Don't Be a D*ck:
Humility and Compassion as
Core Leadership Qualities

"People buy into the leader before they buy into the vision."

– John Maxwell

As organizations navigate the complexities of modern challenges, leaders who embody certain traits cultivate environments where collaboration and innovation can flourish. Humility allows leaders to recognize their limitations, embrace feedback, and prioritize the collective over the individual. This self-awareness not only enhances their decision-making but also fosters trust among team members, makes everyone feels valued and empowered to contribute.

Compassion transcends mere empathy; it drives leaders to take meaningful action in support of their teams and communities. A compassionate leader understands the struggles and aspirations of those around them, facilitating an atmosphere of support and understanding. This quality helps to bridge gaps, resolve conflicts, and inspire loyalty, as team members feel genuinely cared for and understood. In times of uncertainty, leaders who demonstrate compassion can motivate their teams to persevere, reinforcing a strong sense of purpose and belonging.

Together, humility and compassion not only enhance a leader's effectiveness but also shape the overall health of an organization. By prioritizing these qualities, leaders can create a legacy that extends beyond financial success, fostering a culture rooted in mutual respect and shared goals. As we explore the intricacies of these traits, we will examine how they can transform leadership practices and inspire future generations to lead with integrity and heart.

Traits of Terrible Business Leaders

Most people who have worked in a business for a period of time can identify a leader who embodied at least one of these negative traits:

Lack of Empathy

Terrible business leaders often do not try to understand or connect with the emotions and experiences of their team members. They may focus solely on tasks and outputs, treating employees as interchangeable parts rather than people with unique perspectives, challenges, and needs. This lack of empathy leads to a work environment where employees feel unseen and unheard, which can quickly erode morale and trust.

When leaders fail to empathize, they miss critical opportunities to support and motivate their teams. They may overlook signs of burnout, ignore feedback, or dismiss personal concerns that impact performance. Over time, this emotional disconnect can result in higher turnover, lower engagement, and a toxic workplace culture that stifles both well-being and productivity.

Authoritarian Leadership Style

Authoritarian leaders tend to rule with an iron fist, making decisions unilaterally and disregarding the input or insights of their teams. They may believe that their authority is absolute and that questioning their decisions is a sign of disloyalty. While this approach may offer short-term efficiency, it often silences innovation and undermines employee morale.

In environments dominated by authoritarian leadership, team members are often afraid to speak up or challenge the status quo. Creativity, collaboration, and initiative dwindle, as employees focus on avoiding conflict rather than contributing ideas. Over time, this leadership style creates a rigid, fearful culture that struggles to adapt or grow.

Poor Communication Skills

Clear, honest, and consistent communication is the backbone of effective leadership—yet terrible leaders often lack these skills. They may be vague in their expectations, inconsistent in their messaging, or condescending in tone. This creates confusion and frustration, leaving employees unsure of their priorities or how to meet expectations.

Additionally, poor communication contributes to misunderstandings, project delays, and a lack of cohesion within teams. When leaders fail to convey their vision or offer constructive feedback, employees may disengage, feel isolated, or become demoralized. Ineffective communication doesn't just hinder productivity, it also damages relationships and trust within the organization.

Inability to Accept Feedback

Ineffective leaders often operate with a sense of arrogance that makes them resistant to feedback. They may view suggestions or constructive criticism as personal attacks rather than opportunities for improvement. This defensiveness stifles growth, both for the leader and their organization.

By refusing to listen, such leaders isolate themselves from valuable perspectives and insights that could improve decision-making. Over time, their unwillingness to adapt or acknowledge mistakes can result in poor performance, disillusioned employees, and missed opportunities. Effective leadership requires humility—something toxic leaders often lack.

Micromanagement

Leaders who micromanage believe that nothing will be done correctly unless they personally oversee every step. This excessive control undermines employee autonomy and signals a lack of trust. Rather than empowering team members, micromanagers create an environment of anxiety and doubt.

Micromanagement also stifles creativity and slows down processes, as employees are constantly seeking approval for even minor decisions. The result is burnout, resentment, and diminished engagement. Over time, capable employees may leave for roles where they are trusted and respected, leaving the organization with only those willing to tolerate constant oversight.

Blame Game Mentality

When things go wrong, ineffective leaders often look for someone to blame instead of taking responsibility. This behavior not only damages team morale but also creates a culture of fear and blame. Employees may become more focused on self-preservation than collaboration or innovation.

A leader who refuses to acknowledge their mistakes fails to model accountability—an essential trait for high-performing teams. Over time, the blame game erodes psychological safety, discouraging employees from taking initiative or proposing new ideas. It becomes nearly impossible to build a culture of learning and growth when people are afraid of being scapegoated.

Favoritism and Nepotism

Favoritism and nepotism in leadership can quickly erode trust and unity within a team. When promotions, recognition, or opportunities are based on personal relationships rather than merit, it sends a clear message that fairness is not valued. Talented employees who feel overlooked are likely to disengage or leave.

This preferential treatment also undermines team dynamics, breeding resentment and division. It can create an unhealthy competition among employees and reduce collaboration, as individuals may feel they are not playing on an even field. Long-term, it harms both morale and performance, weakening the overall effectiveness of the organization.

Short-Term Focus

Ineffective leaders often prioritize immediate results over sustainable growth. They may chase quick wins, such as cost-cutting or inflated sales tactics, without considering the long-term consequences. This short-sightedness can lead to temporary success, followed by deeper systemic issues.

Organizations led by short-term thinkers often struggle with instability, constant crisis management, and poor strategic planning. Investments in people, innovation, and infrastructure are often neglected, creating a cycle of reaction rather than proactivity. Eventually, the lack of foresight catches up, and the business may find itself unable to compete or evolve.

Lack of Vision

Without a clear and inspiring vision, leaders leave their teams without a sense of purpose or direction. Ineffective leaders often react to problems rather than anticipate them, resulting in a lack of strategic consistency. Employees may feel they are spinning their wheels with no clear destination in sight.

A leader without vision also fails to inspire or rally their team around a shared goal. This leads to disengagement, low morale, and missed opportunities for innovation. Without a guiding vision, decision-making becomes fragmented, and teams struggle to understand how their efforts contribute to a larger mission.

Playing Favorites

Beyond basic favoritism, some ineffective leaders actively create negative competition between employees by pitting them against one another. They may praise certain team members disproportionately or give exclusive access to information and resources. This toxic behavior fosters resentment, cliques, and distrust.

Such dynamics discourage teamwork and promote a toxic culture, where collaboration surrenders to individual survival. Talented employees may grow disillusioned, knowing that their contributions won't be fairly recognized. Over time, this erodes both performance and workplace culture.

Inflexibility

In today's fast-changing business environment, flexibility is essential; yet ineffective leaders often cling to the past, resisting change, dismissing new ideas, and discouraging innovation. This rigidity prevents organizations from evolving with market trends, customer needs, or technological advances.

An inflexible leader not only hinders progress but also frustrates employees who are eager to try new approaches or improve processes. When team members feel stifled, innovation dries up and growth stalls. Inflexibility is not a sign of strength, but a dangerous weakness in a dynamic business landscape.

Dishonesty and Lack of Integrity

A lack of integrity in leadership can poison an entire organization. Leaders who engage in dishonest behavior—whether through misinformation, manipulation, or unethical decisions—undermine trust at every level. Employees may question motives, second-guess decisions, and disengage from the mission.

Trust, once broken, is difficult to rebuild. Teams led by dishonest individuals tend to suffer from low morale, high turnover, and reputational damage that extends beyond internal culture. Ultimately, without integrity, even the most talented teams and sound strategies will struggle to succeed.

Ignoring Employee Well-Being

Ineffective leaders often prioritize productivity and profit at the expense of employee well-being. They may expect long hours, dismiss concerns about burnout, or create environments where mental health is stigmatized. This neglect can have serious consequences for morale, retention, and overall performance.

When employees feel like disposable resources, they begin to engage less. A lack of attention to their well-being leads to increased absenteeism, turnover, and workplace dissatisfaction. Forward-thinking leaders recognize that a healthy team is a productive one, and ignoring this truth is a critical failure.

Resistance to Diversity and Inclusion

Some leaders fail to see the value of a diverse and inclusive workplace, instead hiring and promoting people who mirror their own backgrounds or perspectives. This results in a homogenous culture where innovation and creativity are stifled, and many voices go unheard.

Ignoring diversity also sends a message that the organization is not welcoming or equitable. Talented individuals from underrepresented groups may feel unwelcome or excluded, leading to higher attrition and a damaged brand reputation. Embracing diversity is not only ethically sound—it's a business imperative that ineffective leaders often miss.

Overconfidence and Hubris

Ineffective leaders often believe they are the smartest in the room, regardless of the situation. This overconfidence blinds them to risk, silences dissenting voices, and leads to poor decision-making. When ego overrides humility, the organization suffers.

Hubris also prevents leaders from learning or adapting. They may double down on failing strategies or ignore market signals, believing their intuition is infallible. This mindset not only puts the business at risk but also alienates the very people who could offer solutions and insight.

The Essence of Humility

Humility is often misunderstood in leadership. It's wrongly understood as the quality of minimizing oneself or avoiding recognition. In reality, it's about having an accurate view of your strengths and limitations, while valuing the strengths and contributions of others. Humble leaders are grounded and self-aware. They are secure enough in who they are that they don't need to dominate every conversation or always be right. Instead, they focus on lifting others up and creating space for collaboration and shared success.

This quality allows leaders to build trust and credibility with their teams. When a leader is humble, team members feel safe offering input, asking questions, or admitting mistakes—because their leader models the same behavior. Humility also opens the door for continual growth. Leaders who are open to learning and evolving, who admit they don't have all the answers, can adapt more effectively in complex and changing environments.

The Humble Leader

Satya Nadella, the CEO of Microsoft, exemplifies humility in action. When he took over the role, Microsoft was seen as rigid, internally competitive, and struggling to stay relevant in an evolving tech world. Rather than pretending to have all the answers or clinging to past strategies, Nadella took a different approach. He focused on listening, learning, and building a culture around empathy and growth. By acknowledging the company's missteps and emphasizing a shift from a "know-it-all" to a "learn-it-all" culture, he modeled what it means to lead with humility.

Under his leadership, Microsoft reemerged as an innovation powerhouse, in part because Nadella empowered employees at all levels to contribute. He demonstrated that admitting vulnerability and seeking input isn't a liability but a strategic asset. His ability to be both confident and humble redefined what effective leadership looked like in a company of Microsoft's scale and influence. It's a reminder that humility is not just a moral virtue; it's a business advantage.

Humility in Practice

In day-to-day operations, humility shows up in small but meaningful ways. A humble leader does not dominate meetings—they ask thoughtful questions, invite differing opinions, and credit others for their contributions. They are open to being wrong and see feedback not as criticism, but as a tool for growth. By doing so, they create a psychologically safe space where team members feel empowered to speak up and contribute fully.

Moreover, humble leaders are more likely to admit mistakes and course-correct when needed. This behavior sets a powerful tone for the rest of the organization. Instead of finger-pointing or defensiveness, teams under humble leaders tend to focus on solutions and continuous improvement. In this kind of environment, learning is prioritized over ego, and the collective mission becomes more important than individual recognition.

The Heart of Compassion

Compassion in leadership extends beyond simply understanding others—it involves taking action to support and uplift them. Compassionate leaders are attuned to the needs and emotions of their team members and make decisions with empathy and care. This leadership style recognizes that employees are human beings first—not just units of productivity—and that addressing their emotional and psychological needs is essential for a thriving organization.

True compassion requires intentional effort. It may involve checking in on someone during a difficult time, advocating for flexible work arrangements, or simply being present and listening. When leaders lead with compassion, they cultivate loyalty, deepen trust, and strengthen their organization's culture from the inside out. Compassion, when consistently practiced, becomes a powerful force for unity and resilience.

The Compassionate Leader

Howard Schultz, the former CEO of Starbucks, built much of the company's reputation on a foundation of compassion. By referring to employees as "partners," Schultz conveyed a sense of shared ownership and respect. He implemented benefits that were considered unconventional at the time—including healthcare for part-time employees and education support—because he believed that taking care of people was the right thing to do.

This compassionate approach was not merely altruistic—it was also smart business. Schultz understood that when people feel cared for, they care more about their work. This ethos filtered down to every customer interaction and helped Starbucks become one of the most recognized and respected brands in the world. His leadership serves as a reminder that compassion is not just soft; it is strategic, scalable, and essential to long-term success.

Compassion in Action

Compassionate leadership is particularly crucial during times of crisis. Consider the COVID-19 pandemic, which tested the resilience of leaders around the globe. Leaders who approached the crisis with compassion-by prioritizing employee safety, mental health, and well-being-were better equipped to navigate the challenges. For example, companies that adopted flexible work arrangements and mental health resources during the pandemic saw increased loyalty and productivity from their employees.

Compassionate leaders also create safe spaces for open dialogue. By fostering an environment where employees feel valued and heard, leaders can address concerns and challenges proactively. This approach not only enhances team cohesion but also drives innovation, as team members are more likely to share their ideas in a supportive environment.

The Intersection of Humility and Compassion

While humility and compassion are impactful on their own, their real strength lies in their combination. Humble leaders recognize that they do not have all the answers, while compassionate leaders care deeply about the people around them. Together, these traits create leaders who are grounded, people-centered, and deeply trusted. This blend makes space for collaboration, inclusion, and shared ownership of outcomes.

The intersection of these qualities creates a leadership style that is both confident and caring. Leaders who operate from this place are more capable of managing complexity, guiding through uncertainty, and sustaining long-term success. They foster cultures where people feel safe to take risks, share ideas, and support one another, creating the foundation for extraordinary teams and enduring impact.

Building Trust and Loyalty

Trust is the currency of leadership, and exhibiting humility and compassion are among the best ways to earn it. Leaders who are honest about their limitations and show genuine care for their people foster loyalty that goes beyond job descriptions. When team members feel seen, heard, and valued, they become more invested in their work and more committed to the organization's mission.

This kind of trust doesn't just improve morale, it directly affects performance. Loyal employees frequently go the extra mile, collaborate across functions, and stay with the company long-term. In a world where retention and engagement are critical concerns, the trust cultivated by humble, compassionate leadership becomes a major competitive advantage.

Creating a Culture of Inclusion

Humble and compassionate leaders naturally support inclusive workplaces. Humility allows leaders to acknowledge what they don't know and actively seek diverse perspectives. They do not assume they have all the answers or that their viewpoint is superior. Compassion, meanwhile, ensures that those diverse voices are not only invited but genuinely respected and heard.

This inclusive approach has far-reaching benefits. When employees feel that they belong, they're more likely to contribute fully and authentically. Diverse perspectives lead to better decision-making, increased innovation, and a richer, more resilient workplace culture. Humility and compassion are not just moral imperatives, they are essential tools for building teams that thrive in complexity.

Driving Innovation and Resilience

Innovation flourishes in environments where people feel safe to share ideas and take risks. Humble leaders create these environments by admitting they don't have all the answers and by welcoming input from across the organization. Compassionate leaders add another layer, ensuring that even when ideas fail or fall flat, people are supported and encouraged to try again.

During difficult times, this leadership style also fosters resilience. Instead of fear, uncertainty is met with openness and empathy. Teams rally around shared values and mutual support rather than hierarchy and blame. As a result, organizations led by humble, compassionate leaders are more adaptable, more creative, and ultimately, more successful in navigating both opportunities and challenges.

Case Studies: Leaders Who Exemplify Humility and Compassion

To further illustrate the importance of humility and compassion in leadership, let's examine a couple of case studies.

Case Study 1: Paul Polman, Unilever

Paul Polman, former CEO of Unilever, is renowned for his commitment to sustainability and social responsibility. Under his leadership, Unilever adopted a long-term vision that prioritized environmental and social impact over short-term profits. Polman's humility allowed him to recognize that businesses have a responsibility to contribute positively to society. His compassionate approach led to initiatives that improved the lives of millions through sustainable practices, demonstrating that focus on people and the planet can coexist with profitability.

Case Study 2: Jacinda Ardern, Former Prime Minister of New Zealand

Jacinda Ardern is celebrated for her empathetic leadership style, particularly during times of crisis. Her compassionate response to the Christchurch mosque shootings in 2019 showcased her ability to connect with people on a human level. Through empathy, Ardern united the nation and led with grace and strength, reinforcing the idea that compassionate leadership can inspire collective healing and resilience.

The Role of Humility and Compassion in Leadership Development

As organizations strive to cultivate the next generation of effective leaders, humility and compassion must become central pillars of leadership development. Historically, leadership training has emphasized hard skills, strategic thinking, financial acumen, and operational execution, while overlooking the softer, interpersonal qualities that drive trust, engagement, and long-term success. In today's complex and fast-paced work environment, emotional intelligence and ethical leadership are more critical than ever.

Humility and compassion allow leaders to build meaningful relationships, navigate conflict constructively, and lead with authenticity. These traits are especially vital as companies embrace flatter hierarchies, remote teams, and diverse global workforces. Leaders who can understand others, admit mistakes, and respond with empathy are better equipped to inspire, retain talent, and drive innovation. By embedding these values into leadership development frameworks, organizations can foster more resilient, adaptable, and human-centered leadership cultures.

Training and Development Programs

To effectively integrate humility and compassion into leadership development, organizations must go beyond traditional training formats. Programs should include workshops and experiential learning opportunities that focus on self-awareness, emotional intelligence, and active listening. Role-playing difficult conversations, engaging in empathy-building exercises, and reflecting on personal leadership journeys can help participants better understand the real-world application of these values. These programs should challenge leaders to step out of their comfort zones and explore their blind spots with openness and vulnerability.

Mentorship and peer-coaching can also play a vital role in developing these traits. Pairing emerging leaders with experienced mentors who model humility and compassion allows for a transfer of not only knowledge but also character. When leaders witness these behaviors in action—such as how a mentor handles failure, gives credit, or supports others during adversity—they internalize those lessons more deeply. Over time, these experiences reinforce the belief that leadership is not about control, but about connection and service.

Performance Metrics

Measuring humility and compassion may seem intangible at first glance, but it is both possible and necessary to incorporate these qualities into leadership evaluations. Traditional performance metrics often focus on revenue targets, project completion, or operational efficiency. While these are important, they don't capture the full picture of a leader's impact. Organizations must broaden their evaluation criteria to include indicators such as team morale, collaboration, psychological safety, and employee development, all of which are directly influenced by humble, compassionate leadership.

360-degree feedback tools, employee engagement surveys, and pulse checks can help capture how a leader is perceived by their peers and direct reports. Recognizing and rewarding those who lead with empathy and humility sends a powerful message about what the organization truly values. Over time, these recognition systems shift cultural norms, reinforcing the idea that emotional intelligence is not just a bonus, it's a core competency. When compassion and humility are seen as essential for success, more leaders will strive to embody them, creating a ripple effect across teams and departments.

In summary, humility and compassion are not merely desirable qualities in leadership; they are essential for creating effective, resilient, and innovative organizations. Leaders who embody these traits inspire trust, loyalty, and collaboration within their teams. They cultivate inclusive cultures that empower individuals to contribute their best, driving organizational success.

In contrast, business leaders who embody negative behaviors can have a profound negative effect on their organizations. From a lack of empathy to dishonesty and micromanagement, these characteristics create toxic work environments that stifle innovation, drive away talented employees, and ultimately hinder business success. Recognizing and addressing these negative traits is essential for cultivating a healthier, more productive business environment.

As we move forward in an increasingly complex and interconnected world, the need for leaders who prioritize humility and compassion has never been greater. By embracing these qualities, leaders can navigate challenges with grace, foster meaningful connections, and create lasting positive change in their organizations and communities. The journey of leadership is not just about achieving goals; it is about uplifting others along the way, and in doing so, leaving a legacy of compassion and humility that transcends personal achievements.

Even the most compassionate and humble leaders must eventually face moments of intense pressure—situations where the stakes are high, time is limited, and failure carries profound consequences. It is in these moments that leadership is truly tested. The story of *Apollo 13* offers one of the most compelling examples of crisis leadership; where quick thinking, teamwork, and unwavering resolve turned near-disaster into triumph. In the next chapter, we explore how the mindset of "failure is not an option" reveals the power of calm, focused leadership under pressure—and how the ability to adapt, lead decisively, and persevere through uncertainty remains one of the most vital traits of effective leadership today.

Chapter 8

Failure is not an Option: Leadership Lessons from Apollo 13

"Face reality as it is, not as it was or as you wish it to be."

–Jack Welch

The Apollo 13 mission, launched on April 11, 1970, was the third intended manned lunar landing by NASA. However, it became renowned for its near-disaster and the remarkable rescue efforts that followed. The mission's crew consisted of Commander Jim Lovell, Command Module Pilot Jack Swigert, and Lunar Pilot Fred Haise.

Two days into the mission, while en route to the Moon, an oxygen tank in the service module exploded. This catastrophic event severely crippled the spacecraft, leading to a loss of electrical power and critical life-support systems. The explosion forced the crew to abort their lunar landing and focus entirely on returning safely to Earth.

The astronauts quickly adapted to their new situation, using the Lunar Module, which was designed for landing on the Moon, as a lifeboat. The Lunar Module had limited resources, and the crew faced numerous challenges, including dwindling power and water supplies. Ground control in Houston, Texas, led by flight director Gene Kranz, worked tirelessly with the astronauts to devise strategies for survival and safe re-entry.

The mission highlighted the ingenuity and teamwork of NASA's engineers and scientists. They developed innovative solutions, such as creating a makeshift carbon dioxide scrubber to ensure the crew could breathe. The mission's success relied heavily on collaboration between the crew and the ground team.

After a tense journey, Apollo 13 safely re-entered Earth's atmosphere on April 17, 1970, splashing down in the Pacific Ocean. The mission, while not achieving its original goal of landing on the Moon, became a testament to human resilience and ingenuity, showcasing how challenges can be overcome through teamwork and quick thinking. It remains one of NASA's most famous missions, illustrating the unpredictable nature of space exploration, and emphasizing the importance of problem-solving under pressure.

Jim Lovell

Jim Lovell is a renowned American astronaut and naval aviator, best known for his role in several significant NASA missions, including Apollo 8 and Apollo 13.

Born March 25, 1928, in Milwaukee, Wisconsin, Jim Lovell graduated from the University of Wisconsin-Madison in 1952 with a degree in electrical engineering. Lovell went on to serve as a pilot in the United States Navy and flew missions during the Korean War. He was later assigned to test pilot school, where he honed his skills in aviation.

Lovell later joined NASA and flew on Gemini 7 during its historic mission in December 1965, showcasing exceptional leadership and piloting skills. This mission, notable for its long duration of nearly 14 days, aimed to test the endurance of astronauts in space and gather vital data for experiments and maneuvers, including the first space rendezvous with Gemini 6. Lovell's calm demeanor and problem-solving abilities were crucial in navigating challenges.

Jim Lovell commanded Gemini 12 in November 1966, leading a pivotal mission that aimed to demonstrate the effectiveness of spacewalks and the techniques necessary for future Apollo lunar landings. Alongside astronaut Edwin "Buzz" Aldrin, Lovell executed a series of complex tasks, including successful extravehicular activities (EVAs) that showcased new methods for astronauts to work outside the spacecraft. The mission achieved significant milestones, such as the longest duration of a spaceflight up until that point and a successful rendezvous with another spacecraft. Lovell's adept leadership and collaborative spirit were crucial in overcoming challenges, ultimately contributing valuable data to the United States space program and enhancing the understanding of human capabilities in space.

In December 1968, Lovell commanded Apollo 8, which marked the first time humans orbited the Moon. Alongside crewmates Frank Borman and William Anders, Lovell led the spacecraft on a historic journey that showcased NASA's capabilities and provided critical insights for future lunar exploration. The mission involved a series of complex maneuvers, including a successful trans-lunar injection and lunar orbit insertion. Lovell's leadership and calmness under pressure were instrumental in navigating challenges, including a critical engine burn that ensured their safe return to Earth. Apollo 8's iconic Christmas Eve broadcast, featuring stunning views of the Earth and Moon, inspired millions and solidified Lovell's legacy as a pioneering figure in space exploration.

In April 1970, Lovell commanded Apollo 13, which suffered a critical failure en route to the Moon. The phrase, "Houston, we have a problem" became iconic as Lovell and his crew worked with mission control to safely return to Earth. The successful rescue operation turned a potential tragedy into a story of ingenuity and teamwork.

Gene Krantz

Gene Kranz is a prominent figure in NASA's history, known for his leadership during the Apollo missions, particularly Apollo 11, which landed the first humans on the Moon in 1969. Born on August 17, 1933, in Toledo, Ohio, Kranz earned a degree in aeronautical engineering from the United States Air Force Academy and served as a fighter pilot before joining NASA.

Kranz joined NASA in 1960, initially working as a flight controller. He quickly rose through the ranks because of his expertise and leadership skills. He became known for his no-nonsense approach and his ability to remain calm under pressure. His pivotal role came during the Apollo missions, where he served as the Flight Director during several critical flights, including the ill-fated Apollo 13 mission in 1970.

During Apollo 13, when an oxygen tank exploded en route to the Moon, Kranz and his team were instrumental in devising a plan to safely return the astronauts to Earth, showcasing their problem-solving skills and teamwork. His famous quote, "failure is not an option," has become synonymous with NASA's commitment to excellence.

Leadership Lessons from Apollo 13

Agility–Having the capability to adapt and innovate based on the changing environment without losing momentum.

The Apollo 13 mission is often remembered not for its intended lunar landing, but for the breathtaking recovery that turned a near-catastrophe into one of history's most celebrated examples of leadership, collaboration, and ingenuity. What unfolded over the course of those tense days in April 1970 was not just a feat of engineering—it was a case study in human-centered leadership. The crisis offered a blueprint for navigating uncertainty with clarity, calm, and courage. The following lessons, drawn from the Apollo 13 mission, remain profoundly relevant for today's leaders who must guide teams through their own high-stakes, high-pressure situations.

One of the most powerful qualities demonstrated during the mission was the ability to **stay calm under pressure**. When an oxygen tank exploded mid-flight, chaos could have easily taken over. But at NASA's Mission Control in Houston, Flight Director Gene Kranz didn't allow panic to win. Instead, he centered his team with the now-iconic instruction: *"Let's work the problem."* His steadiness became contagious. In that moment, calm wasn't just a leadership trait—it was a lifeline. In today's boardrooms and crisis rooms, leaders who can steady their teams during moments of uncertainty are better equipped to move forward with clarity and confidence. Calm doesn't mean emotionless—it means choosing focus over fear when it matters most.

As the crisis unfolded, it became clear that no individual could solve it alone. The rescue became a triumph of **collaborative problem-solving**, with hundreds of engineers and scientists working around the clock to devise solutions—often using nothing more than the tools and materials available onboard the spacecraft. This culture of collaboration was not accidental; it had been fostered long before launch. Effective leaders don't wait for a crisis to create teamwork—they build it into the DNA of their organizations. They invite diverse perspectives, encourage questions, and value contribution over rank. What Apollo 13 revealed was that ingenuity flourishes when hierarchy does not supersede all else, and every voice is valued.

Adaptability rose to the forefront once it was clear that the original mission, landing on the Moon, was no longer possible. The crew had to pivot rapidly, using the Lunar Module as a lifeboat and recalculating every step of their return to Earth. This level of flexibility required trust and quick thinking across multiple teams. In leadership today, the same principle holds: when plans unravel, leaders must pivot without hesitation. Stubbornly clinging to outdated strategies can sink even the most talented teams. Agile leaders, by contrast, know when to shift focus, realign resources, and keep their teams moving forward, even when the destination changes.

Despite the enormity of the situation, the NASA team maintained a **relentless focus on the mission**: bringing the astronauts home safely. That singular objective became the rallying point for every decision, every calculation, every moment of tension. In modern leadership, that kind of focus is critical. Distractions, pressures, and competing priorities can easily fracture a team's energy. But when a leader articulates a clear mission—and returns to it consistently—it provides a stabilizing force that unites effort and inspires persistence.

Another defining aspect of Apollo 13 was the way leadership was **shared and empowered**. Commander Jim Lovell didn't merely give orders, he encouraged his crew and the ground teams to think creatively, to speak up, and to own their part of the solution. Empowerment was not just nice to have—it was necessary for survival. In today's world, where complex challenges require fast, decentralized decision-making, the ability to empower teams is a leadership superpower. Leaders who trust their people to lead from where they are, build more resilient, capable organizations.

Much of the success of Apollo 13 can also be traced back to what happened *before* the launch. **Preparation** was everything. The astronauts and ground teams had trained for countless failure scenarios. Simulations were grueling and often repetitive, but they laid the groundwork for quick thinking under pressure. Leaders today often look to innovation or agility as competitive advantages—but preparation is just as critical. Whether through crisis simulations, strategic planning, or mentorship, equipping teams to handle adversity before it arrives creates the conditions for excellence when stakes are high.

Communication, too, was non-negotiable. Lives depended on clear, direct, and unambiguous instructions between the spacecraft and Mission Control. There was no room for confusion or ego—only clarity. Today's leaders must communicate with similar discipline. In moments of pressure, teams look to their leaders not just for guidance, but for assurance. Listening is just as important in effective communication as speaking. Leaders who encourage open dialogue, who hear concerns and invite feedback, cultivate cultures where people feel both safe and seen.

And while the mission did not fulfill its original goal, it became a powerful reminder of the importance of **learning from failure**. The experience shaped how NASA approached future missions, leading to major improvements in spacecraft design, risk assessment, and team coordination. Rather than assigning blame, the organization focused on reflection and growth. In business and beyond, leaders who foster a culture where failure is examined, not punished, enable innovation to thrive. It sends a powerful message: what matters is not just what went wrong, but what we learn from it.

The final ingredient behind the Apollo 13 recovery was something less technical but no less vital: **team culture**. What bound everyone together, from astronauts to engineers, was a shared sense of mission and mutual respect. The camaraderie, discipline, and trust had been built long before the crisis hit, and it paid dividends when things went wrong. Today's most successful leaders understand that culture isn't a byproduct of success, it's a prerequisite.

Above all, the mission stands as a testament to **resilience**. The Apollo 13 crew and support teams were knocked off course, literally and figuratively, but never lost their determination. Their ability to improvise, support one another, and remain mission-focused under intense pressure saved lives and inspired millions. In the same way, modern leaders must model resilience, not by pretending adversity doesn't exist, but by showing their teams how to face it with resolve and courage.

The story of Apollo 13 is not simply about survival, it is about leadership at its best. It's about people who stayed calm in chaos, who collaborated without ego, who adapted without hesitation, and who never lost sight of their mission. These aren't just lessons from space, they are tools for earthbound leaders striving to navigate complexity with character, clarity, and courage.

The leadership lessons from Apollo 13 extend far beyond the realm of space exploration. The principles of calmness, collaboration, and adaptability, focus, empowerment, preparation, communication, learning from failure, team culture, and resilience are applicable in various contexts, from corporate environments to community organizations.

By adopting these lessons, leaders can navigate challenges and inspire their team to achieve remarkable outcomes, even in the face of adversity. The story of Apollo 13 serves as a powerful reminder of the potential for human ingenuity and teamwork in overcoming even the most daunting obstacles. As leaders reflect on the lessons from this mission, they can cultivate a culture of excellence, resilience, and unity within their organizations, ultimately leading to greater success and fulfillment.

While Apollo 13 showcased the extraordinary power of resilience and problem-solving under pressure, it also highlights a deeper truth: success doesn't always look like the original plan. In leadership, the path forward is rarely linear, and the ability to pivot with purpose is often what separates stagnation from progress. As we turn to the next chapter, we explore how great leaders redefine success in the face of unexpected challenges, shifting their goals, adapting their strategies, and embracing change not as a setback, but as an opportunity for growth, reinvention, and renewed clarity.

Chapter 9

Redefining Success:
The Letter Story

One afternoon, not long after I started with Solari, I was sitting in my office at my computer when I noticed out of the corner of my eye an older, portly gentleman, no more than five foot six, walk through our front door with tears running down his face. Without saying a word, he approached our reception desk, handed the staff member a tattered envelope, turned and walked out.

I was puzzled as the staff member brought the envelope over to me, saying that it was addressed to an employee who no longer worked here asking what she should do with it. I said that it was clearly an emotional situation, and then the man went through the effort of bringing the letter all the way to our office. We should probably open it to see what was inside.

As I opened the envelope and read the first line, my heart dropped, and I got a vast pit in my stomach… 'This will not be a good letter,' I said to the team member.

Dear Robert,

Today marks the first anniversary of my daughter's death by suicide.

My daughter struggled her entire life with mental health and substance abuse issues. She battled the demons in her head each and every day however she could. Sometimes with her medication, sometimes with therapy, and other times with drugs or alcohol. Her depression was crippling and the desire to die was a constant struggle. She went in and out of hospitals and treatment programs, but never found the help and support she needed. It was tearing my family apart.

Three years ago, around Christmas, she was having another episode and threatening to take her own life. We convinced her to call the crisis line, as we have done many times before, and you picked up the phone. I'm sure this was one of many unremarkable calls you take in a day, but please know that you changed our lives that night.

I'm not sure what it was about you or the conversation you had with her, but something changed, something clicked with my daughter. Somehow you sparked a light in her that I've never seen before. No one had ever made an impact on her like you did that night. No hospital, no doctor, no therapy group, not even her family. It was you.

After the call, she had something that she never had before: Hope.

She was hopeful and excited about the future! She started taking her medication again, going to groups, getting out of her room, and connecting with her friends and family.

Though she ultimately succumbed to her illness, we had the BEST two years with her... thanks to you.

As I mourn the anniversary of her death, I am grateful that you picked up the phone that night and blessed us with the gift of two years that I believe we wouldn't have had without your help.

Sincerely,

- A grieving father

This letter has had a profound effect on me personally as well as in my role as a leader. My preconceived notions of success in this father's shoes did not include his daughter's death at a tragically young age. I have had to reconcile within myself the fact that success can look a lot of different ways. We may hit a roadblock in what we initially set out to accomplish that requires us to pivot, redefine what success looks like, and move forward.

In the realm of business, success is often celebrated through the lens of financial metrics–revenue growth, profit margins, and market share. However, this narrow definition fails to capture the diverse and nuanced ways that success can manifest across different organizations and industries. Success in business is not a one-size-fits-all concept; it is shaped by individual company values, stakeholder expectations, and the unique challenges faced within specific contexts. This chapter explores the multifaceted nature of success in business, presenting various definitions and illustrating how these definitions can affect organizational strategies and outcomes.

1. Financial Success

The most conventional definition of success in business revolves around financial performance. Metrics such as revenue, profit, and return on investment (ROI) are standard indicators used by investors, board members, and analysts to assess a company's viability and growth potential. For instance, publicly traded companies are frequently evaluated based on their quarterly earnings report. Firms like Apple and Google are often lauded for their impressive financial results, which serve as a testament to their market dominance and operational efficiency.

Financial success is significant, yet limited. A singular focus on profit can lead to short-term thinking, where businesses prioritize immediate gains over long-term sustainability. This myopic view can result in cost-cutting measures that compromise product quality, employee well-being, and customer satisfaction. For example, companies that aggressively reduce labor costs to boost profits may experience high turnover, decreased morale, and, ultimately, a tarnished brand reputation.

2. Customer Satisfaction

Another vital measure of success is customer satisfaction. Businesses that prioritize delivering exceptional customer experiences often enjoy better loyalty and retention rates. In today's competitive landscape where consumers have numerous choices, a positive customer experience can be a key differentiator. Companies like Amazon and Zappos have gained recognition for their commitment to customer service, demonstrating that success can be defined by the ability to meet and exceed customer expectations.

To gauge customer satisfaction, businesses can employ various metrics, such as Net Promoter Score (NPS), Customer Satisfaction Score (CSAT), and Customer Effort Score (CES). These indicators help organizations understand how well they are meeting customer needs and identify areas for improvement. Companies that embrace a customer-centric approach often find that more satisfied customers lead to increased referrals and repeat business, ultimately contributing to long-term success.

3. Employee Well-Being

A growing number of businesses define success through the lens of employee well-being. Companies that invest in their workforce by promoting a positive culture and ensuring work-life balance often see increased productivity and lower turnover rates. Organizations like Google and Salesforce exemplify this approach, emphasizing the importance of employee happiness and engagement as vital components of their success.

To foster employee well-being, organizations can implement policies that support mental health, provide opportunities for professional development, and promote work-life balance. For instance, offering flexible work hours and remote work options can help employees manage personal responsibilities alongside their professional obligations. When employees feel valued and supported, they are more likely to be motivated and invested in their work, leading to improved outcomes for the organization.

4. Social Impact

In recent years, many businesses have begun to define success not just by financial metrics but by their social impact. Companies like TOMS and Patagonia focus on sustainability and ethical practices, demonstrating that profit can coexist with a commitment to social responsibility. This shift reflects a growing consumer preference for brands that align with their values, making social impact an essential component of modern business success.

To assess social impact, businesses can establish metrics that track their contributions to community welfare, environmental sustainability, and ethical governance. For instance, B Corporations are certified based on their social and environmental performance and are held accountable to higher standards of transparency and accountability. As consumers increasingly demand social responsibility from brands, organizations that prioritize their social impact can achieve a competitive advantage in the marketplace.

5. Innovation and Creativity

In dynamic industries, success can also be defined by innovation. Companies that prioritize research and development, foster creativity, and embrace change often lead their markets. Organizations like Tesla exemplify this definition of success, as they continuously push boundaries and reimagine what is possible within the automotive industry.

To cultivate a culture of innovation, organizations must encourage risk-taking and experimentation. This can be achieved by creating spaces for collaboration, providing resources for research and development, and celebrating creative ideas, even if they do not lead to immediate success. Companies that foster a spirit of innovation not only stay ahead of competitors but also attract top talent eager to work in forward-thinking environments.

6. Market Positioning

Some businesses define success based on their market positioning and brand reputation. A powerful brand that resonates with its audience can achieve success even without dominating the market. Luxury brands like Chanel and Rolex succeed by cultivating exclusivity and a strong identity, focusing on brand perception rather than sheer volume of sales.

To build brand equity, organizations must consistently deliver on their brand promise and create emotional connections with customers. This can involve storytelling, strategic marketing, and delivering exceptional experiences that align with the brand's values. Companies that effectively manage their brand reputation can maintain customer loyalty and command premium pricing, contributing to long-term success.

7. Adaptability and Resilience

In an ever-changing business landscape, adaptability is crucial. Companies that can pivot in response to market demands or crises often define their success by their resilience. The COVID-19 pandemic showcased businesses that successfully adapted to remote work and digital transformations, illustrating that flexibility is a key component of success.

To enhance adaptability, organizations can implement agile methodologies, prioritize continuous learning, and encourage cross-functional collaboration. By fostering a culture that embraces change and encourages experimentation, businesses can better navigate uncertainties and seize new opportunities. Companies that remain resilient in the face of challenges often emerge stronger and more successful.

8. Long-Term Vision

Finally, some organizations measure success by their long-term vision and sustainability. Companies that focus on building a legacy and prioritizing future generations may define success by their lasting impact rather than immediate gains. This approach is often seen in family-owned businesses that strive to maintain their values and mission across generations.

To achieve long-term success, organizations must create a strategic vision that aligns with their values and goals. This involves setting measurable objectives, investing in talent development, and developing sustainable practices that consider future generations. Businesses that prioritize long-term success can build resilience, adaptability, and a positive reputation, securing their relevance in a changing world.

A Case Study: Horizon Books

Founded in the late 1990s, Horizon Books began as a chain of independent bookstores dedicated to offering a curated literary experience in an era where big-box retailers were rapidly dominating the market. For its first decade, the company measured success in traditional terms—store expansion, sales growth, and inventory turnover. But by the early 2010s, Horizon faced mounting challenges: the rise of e-commerce giants, changing reading habits, and the decline of physical retail. With profits slipping and store closures looming, the leadership team faced a difficult question, should they double down on their old model, or redefine what success looked like?

Rather than competing on price or volume, Horizon chose to pivot, radically. The leadership recognized that their core value wasn't just selling books, but building community through storytelling, education, and connection. They reimagined their stores not just as retail spaces, but as cultural hubs. Horizon scaled down its inventory and converted parts of its stores into reading lounges, event spaces, and coworking areas. They launched programs that offered free literary workshops, book clubs, author meetups, and after-school reading sessions for underserved youth.

Simultaneously, Horizon invested in local partnerships, collaborating with schools, libraries, and community organizations to bring books and literacy programs into neighborhoods that lacked access. They also introduced a curated subscription service that matched readers with independent authors, reinforcing their commitment to discovering and supporting emerging voices in literature.

Though this pivot meant slower revenue growth at first, Horizon's redefined success began to show dividends in other ways. Foot traffic increased. Communities rallied around the stores. Customer loyalty deepened. Horizon's brand was no longer about competing with online giants, it was about offering something irreplaceable: human connection, local presence, and shared values.

By 2020, Horizon Books had not only stabilized but had earned national attention for its innovative, community-first approach. They became a model for how legacy businesses can remain relevant by letting go of outdated benchmarks and embracing a broader definition of success, one grounded in purpose, impact, and adaptability.

Horizon's story illustrates that when leaders are willing to pivot with intention and humility, they can transform adversity into opportunity. Redefining success isn't about abandoning ambition, it's about aligning it with values that endure beyond market trends.

Success in business is a complex and multifaceted concept that cannot be reduced to a single definition. From financial performance to customer satisfaction, employee well-being, social impact, innovation, market positioning, adaptability, and long-term vision, there are many ways to measure success. As businesses evolve, so too does the definition of success, reflecting the diverse values and priorities of stakeholders in today's complex landscape. Embracing a broader perspective on success can lead to more sustainable and meaningful outcomes for businesses and their communities. Ultimately, recognizing and valuing the different dimensions of success can empower organizations to thrive in an increasingly competitive and dynamic environment.

As organizations embrace a more expansive view of success, another powerful principle emerges: the value of simplicity. In a world overloaded with complexity, information, and constant change, the ability to distill ideas, products, and strategies down to their essence is a rare and transformative skill. Few leaders understood this better than Steve Jobs. In the next chapter, we explore how Jobs harnessed the power of simplicity, not as a design trend, but as a leadership philosophy, to drive innovation, clarity, and focus within Apple, ultimately reshaping industries, and redefining consumer expectations worldwide.

Chapter 10

Keep It Simple, Stupid: The Power of Simplicity in Business

"Simple can be harder than complex, you have to work hard to get your thinking clean to make it simple."

– Steve Jobs

In the world of business, complexity often reigns supreme, with companies bombarding consumers with intricate features and convoluted messaging. However, the power of simplicity cannot be overstated, as it has the potential to cut through the noise and resonate deeply with the audiences. This chapter explores how simplicity stands as a cornerstone of innovation and effectiveness, exemplified by the legendary Steve Jobs and the KISS principle–"Keep It Simple, Stupid." By adhering to these principles, businesses can enhance clarity, foster engagement, and drive success in an increasingly complicated world.

The Beauty of Simplicity

Simplicity in business and leadership is the art of distilling complex ideas and processes into clear, actionable components. In a world increasingly overwhelmed by information and choices, simplicity serves as a guiding principle that enhances decision-making. Leaders who embrace simplicity prioritize clarity in communication, ensuring that their teams understand objectives and the rationale behind decisions. This clarity not only boosts morale but also fosters a culture of transparency where employees feel empowered to contribute and innovate.

Simplicity in leadership encourages agility. Organizations that simplify their structures and processes can respond more effectively to changes in the market or internal dynamics. By eliminating unnecessary bureaucracy and focusing on core values and objectives, leaders can streamline operations and enhance productivity. This adaptability is crucial in today's fast-paced business environment, where pivoting quickly can be the difference between success and failure.

Finally, simplicity cultivates a strong connection with customers. Businesses that prioritize straightforward messaging and user-friendly experiences tend to build stronger relationships with their clientele. By focusing on what truly matters–whether it's product quality, customer service, or brand values–companies can resonate more deeply with their audience. Simplicity not only streamlines operations, it also strengthens the bond between a business and its customers, creating a loyal base that drives long-term success.

The KISS Principle

The KISS principle, which stands for "Keep It Simple, Stupid," emphasizes simplicity and clarity, particularly relevant to Alcoholics Anonymous (AA) and other 12-step programs. The foundational philosophy of these programs is to provide individuals struggling with addiction a straightforward pathway to recovery. This simplicity is crucial, as it helps participants focus on the essential steps required to achieve sobriety without becoming overwhelmed by complex theories and jargon. The 12 steps themselves are designed to be easily understood and followed, making recovery accessible to everyone, regardless of their background or level of education.

The KISS principle manifests in the language and structure of the 12-step program. Each step is articulated clearly and concisely, guiding participants through a series of manageable tasks such as admitting powerlessness over alcohol and making amends for past mistakes. This step-by-step approach allows individuals to concentrate on one task at a time, fostering a sense of accomplishment and reducing anxiety.

Using straightforward language in meetings and literature ensures that members feel included and understood, promoting a supportive community where complex feelings and experiences can be shared without fear of judgement.

The KISS principle encourages a focus on personal experience rather than theoretical concepts. In AA meetings, members share their stories in a relatable manner, emphasizing common struggles and victories. This peer support reinforces the idea that recovery is a shared journey, allowing individuals to see that they are not alone in their challenges. By prioritizing simplicity in communication and process, 12-step programs empower participants to engage actively in their recovery, and provide them with a sense of hope and purpose—essential components for long-term sobriety.

The KISS principle is also relevant in the business world where products, services and strategies often become convoluted over time. Simplicity encourages creativity and innovation. When teams focus on simple solutions, they can explore new ideas without being bogged down by layers of complexity. This approach often leads to breakthroughs, allowing businesses to adapt and thrive in a fast-paced environment.

Steve Jobs

Steve Jobs is a quintessential example of how simplicity can drive business success. His belief in the power of simplicity was reflected in every aspect of Apple's products and marketing strategies. Jobs understood that consumers often seek products that are easy to use and understand. He famously stated, "Design is not just what it looks like and feels like. Design is how it works." This encapsulates his vision of simplicity–not just in aesthetics but in functionality.

Jobs was born on February 24, 1955, in San Francisco, California, and was adopted shortly after his birth. He grew up in the suburbs of the Bay Area, where he developed an early interest in electronics and design. Jobs attended Reed College but dropped out after just one semester, choosing instead to explore his interests in technology and spirituality.

In 1976, he co-founded Apple Computer, with Steve Wozniak and Ronald Wayne, launching the Apple I computer, which set the stage for a revolution in personal computing.

Under Jobs's leadership, Apple released several groundbreaking products, including the Macintosh in 1984, which was notable for its graphical user interface. However, after a power struggle within the company, Jobs left Apple in 1985. During his time away, he founded NeXT, a computer platform development company, and acquired Pixar Animation Studios, which became a major player in animated filmmaking. His experiences during this period helped him refine his vision of design and innovation.

In 1997, Jobs returned to an Apple that was mired in financial struggles. He revitalized the brand by focusing on innovative products like the iMac, iPod, iPhone, and iPad, which transformed consumer technology and solidified Apple's status as a leader in the industry. Jobs was known for his intense focus on product design and marketing, as well as his charismatic presentation style. He passed away on October 5, 2011, but left behind a legacy of innovation that continues to influence technology and design today.

The Power of Simplicity

Few leaders have harnessed the power of simplicity as masterfully as Steve Jobs. While many viewed complexity as a sign of sophistication, Jobs saw it as a barrier—to clarity, to innovation, and most importantly, to the customer. For him, simplicity wasn't the absence of complexity; it was the thoughtful, disciplined removal of anything that distracted from the core purpose. From product design to corporate culture, Jobs built simplicity into Apple's DNA, transforming it from a struggling company in the late 1990s into one of the most valuable brands in the world.

Product Design: Elegance in Essentials

Apple's products are synonymous with minimalist beauty—but that aesthetic is deeply functional. The iPhone, perhaps the most iconic example, didn't succeed merely because of its technological prowess; it succeeded because it *felt* simple. At a time when other smartphones were cluttered with buttons, dropdown menus, and cryptic interfaces, Apple presented a sleek rectangle with a single button. No manual required. As Jobs famously said, "It just works."

This philosophy was rooted in the KISS principle—*Keep It Simple, Stupid*—but with a nuance Jobs uniquely understood: simplicity is hard. It requires ruthless clarity about what matters most. He and his team spent countless hours debating what features to remove, not just what to add. Their goal was always the same: to create an experience so intuitive, so seamless, that technology faded into the background. In doing so, they empowered users of all ages and technical skill levels to embrace innovation without fear or friction.

Marketing Strategy: Say Less, Mean More

Jobs did not just apply simplicity to the products; he infused it into Apple's marketing DNA. In an industry known for shouting specs and features, Apple whispered. Their ads featured crisp visuals, clean fonts, and short, punchy taglines. Whether it was "Think Different" or simply a silhouette of someone dancing with an iPod, the message was clear: this product will enhance your life.

By focusing on emotional resonance rather than technical detail, Jobs avoided overwhelming customers with jargon. Instead, he invited them to imagine what was possible. This minimalist approach made Apple's messaging not only more memorable but also more meaningful. It was a stark contrast to competitors who tried to impress with long spec sheets, and it worked. Jobs knew that in a noisy world, simplicity is what cuts through.

Simplicity in Business Processes: Trimming the Fat

Jobs did not just champion simplicity externally, he applied it inside Apple too. After returning to the company in 1997, one of his first moves was to slash Apple's sprawling product line. The message was simple: *do fewer things, better*. That clarity allowed teams to focus, innovate, and move faster.

Under Jobs's leadership, Apple also became a model of operational efficiency. He worked closely with COO Tim Cook to streamline the company's supply chain, turning it into one of the most efficient in the world. Rather than expanding complexity with multiple vendors and distribution models, they centralized key operations. Fewer moving parts meant lower costs, faster delivery, and a better customer experience. It was simplicity in action: quiet, disciplined, and transformative.

Organizational Structure: Fewer Layers, Faster Decisions

At Apple, simplicity extended to structure. Jobs was famously involved in product design decisions, but he did not micromanage. He built lean teams, flattened hierarchies, and empowered individuals with clear mandates. This allowed Apple to move quickly and avoid the bureaucratic drag that slows down larger organizations.

By keeping communication lines open and eliminating unnecessary layers of management, Jobs cultivated a culture where ideas flowed freely and decisions happened quickly. In contrast, companies burdened by complex reporting structures often struggle with inertia. Jobs's approach showed that simplifying structure is not about doing less, it is about enabling more of what matters.

The Customer Experience: Simplicity as a Relationship Builder

For Jobs, the customer experience was sacred, and simplicity was its foundation. Every detail, from the unboxing of a new iPhone to the layout of the Apple Store, was designed with the user in mind. He obsessed over how products felt in the hand, how menus responded to touch, and how quickly someone could find what they needed.

This commitment to simplicity created a sense of ease that translated into loyalty. Apple did not just sell devices—they built relationships. Customers felt understood because Apple had taken the time to remove barriers, confusion, and frustration. In an age of choice overload, Jobs understood that the companies that simplify, win.

Customer Feedback: Listening Without Friction

Jobs's relationship with customers was not always direct, but it was deeply informed. He believed that users often did not know exactly what they wanted, but they knew how they felt. By analyzing behavior, responding to feedback loops, and engaging in subtle iteration, Apple continually refined its products in ways that felt almost intuitive.

Importantly, Apple made it easy to engage, through genius bars, seamless software updates, and responsive support. They did not ask customers to jump through hoops. They met them where they were. Simplicity, in this sense, became a feedback accelerator.

The Competitive Advantage of Simplicity

Jobs understood that in a world filled with noise, simplicity is a strategic advantage. Companies that eliminate friction move faster. They waste less, think clearer, and connect more deeply with their audience. Apple's ability to focus on fewer, better products gave it the flexibility to adapt quickly to market changes, while competitors were bogged down by bloated product lines and unclear messaging.

Simplicity also builds trust. When customers can understand a product at a glance, when pricing is transparent, and when value is immediately apparent, decision-making becomes easier. In an economy where attention is scarce, that clarity is gold.

Creating a Unique Value Proposition: Simplicity as Brand DNA

Apple's brand identity was not built on price or even specs, it was built on experience. Jobs positioned Apple not just as a tech company, but as a lifestyle brand. Their value proposition wasn't *more features*, it was a *better experience*. That distinction became Apple's north star.

This unique position attracted customers who did not just want tools, they wanted beautifully designed, easy-to-use devices that fit seamlessly into their lives. Jobs understood that simplicity was not just a design choice. It was the brand.

Innovation Through Simplicity: Space to Think, Room to Create

Perhaps the most underappreciated power of simplicity is its role in innovation. Complexity clutters the mind. Simplicity clears it. By focusing teams on fewer goals and encouraging clarity of thought, Jobs created an environment where breakthrough ideas could emerge.

He famously said, "Innovation is saying no to 1,000 things." It is a philosophy that continues to drive Apple's success today. Instead of chasing trends or adding layers, Apple refines, refines, and refines, until what is left is elegant, useful, and utterly transformative.

In the End: Simplicity is Sophistication

Steve Jobs once quoted Leonardo da Vinci, saying, *"Simplicity is the ultimate sophistication."* He did not just believe it, he built a legacy on it. For leaders today, Jobs's example is more than a design aesthetic. It is a call to action. In our increasingly complex world, those who can simplify, who can focus on what truly matters, will rise above the noise, inspire loyalty, and lead with clarity.

The value of simplicity in business cannot be overstated. Through the lens of Steve Jobs and the KISS principles, we see that simplicity is not just a design aesthetic but a fundamental business strategy. By embracing simplicity in product design, marketing, processes, and customer experience, companies can enhance innovation, improve efficiency, and create lasting relationships with their customers.

In a world that increasingly values clarity and convenience, businesses that prioritize simplicity will not only survive but thrive. As we move into an era of even more rapid change and complexity, let us remember that the simplest solutions are often the most effective, and that simplicity is a powerful driver of success. By keeping it simple, businesses can navigate the complexities of the market and create meaningful connections with their customers, leading to sustainable growth and success.

As we leave the world of sleek design and minimalist strategy, we now turn to a more grounded metaphor for leadership, one rooted in patience, care, and long-term growth. Just as simplicity clears the way for innovation, cultivating effective leadership requires intention, consistency, and a deep understanding of the environment in which people grow. Much like farming, leadership is not about quick wins or instant results, it is about preparing the soil, planting seeds, nurturing development, and trusting the process. In the next chapter, we explore how the principles of farming can illuminate powerful lessons for leadership, reminding us that great leaders, like great farmers, know when to sow, when to tend, and when to step back and let growth take root.

Chapter 11

Cultivating Leadership: The Intersection of Farming Skills and Business Success

"The farmer has to be an optimist or he wouldn't still be a farmer."

– Will Rogers

A Story of Patience, Resilience, and Stewardship

Leadership Lessons from the Land: Cultivating Growth Like a Farmer

Leadership in the modern world often conjures images of fast-paced boardrooms, digital dashboards, and real-time metrics. But long before agile methodologies and quarterly earnings reports, leadership existed in a quieter, humbler form, in the fields, where farmers rose with the sun and measured progress in seasons, not seconds.

The work of a farmer, at its core, embodies patience, adaptability, and wisdom. Upon closer examination, the parallels between farming and leadership become undeniable. Both require vision and discipline. Both demand a deep understanding of resources, people, and timing. And both are less about control and more about cultivation, knowing when to act, when to wait, and how to nurture growth without forcing it.

This chapter explores how timeless farming practices offer powerful lessons for today's leaders, revealing that the path to sustainable success is not built on speed or scale alone, but on resilience, intentionality, and care.

Weathering the Storm: Resilience and Adaptability

Farming begins with hope, but it endures through uncertainty. One season may bring rain and abundance; the next, drought and loss. Farmers learn early that they cannot control the weather—but they can control how they respond to it.

Consider Mike, a farmer in Kansas who endured one of the worst droughts in a generation. While neighboring farms struggled to survive, Mike adapted. He invested in drought-resistant crops, installed drip irrigation systems, and embraced conservation practices. It was not easy, but it worked. His harvest was smaller, yes, but it was sustainable. More importantly, his soil was healthier, and his methods positioned him for long-term success.

In the business world, the storms take different forms, market disruptions, economic downturns, technological shifts. But the need for resilience is the same. Leaders must be able to absorb the shock, recalibrate quickly, and lead their teams with clarity and confidence through the chaos. Resilient leaders don't collapse when things go wrong, they bend, adapt, and grow stronger.

Sowing the Future: Long-Term Vision and Planning

Every farmer knows that what you sow in spring determines what you reap in fall. The decisions made today, what to plant, when to plant, where to rotate, must take into account not just the current season, but seasons to come. This long-range thinking is central to farming, and it is just as vital in leadership.

Great leaders don't chase only short-term wins; they cultivate a vision that stretches years into the future. They ask not just, "What do we want to achieve this quarter?" but, "Where do we want to be a decade from now?" Like a farmer planning crop rotations to preserve soil health, leaders make strategic decisions that ensure the well-being and sustainability of their organizations.

Consider a renewable energy firm with a ten-year vision to become a market leader in solar technology. Its leadership does not merely focus on product launches or quarterly profits, they develop roadmaps that include research, partnerships, policy advocacy, and talent development. By mapping out that long-term journey, they turn vision into momentum.

Harvesting Potential: Resource Management

A farmer's livelihood depends on using every resource, land, water, labor, tools, with precision and care. Waste is costly. Overuse is dangerous. Every decision is a balancing act: how to maximize yield without depleting the soil, how to meet demand without compromising sustainability.

Business leaders face similar challenges. Whether managing capital, human talent, or time, they must be shrewd stewards of what they have. The best leaders do not just allocate, they cultivate. They invest in their people, cross-train their teams, streamline operations, and find new ways to do more with less.

When supply chains are disrupted or budgets tighten, it is resourceful leaders who find alternatives, shift strategies, and maintain productivity without burning out their teams. Like farmers who adapt to a changing climate, these leaders are constantly refining how they use what they have to meet evolving needs.

The Power of the Collective: Teamwork and Community

Out in the fields, collaboration is not optional, it is essential. Neighbors share equipment, exchange knowledge, and lend helping hands during harvest. Farming may be solitary at times, but the success of a community often depends on its ability to work together.

In leadership, the same truth applies: the lone genius myth is just that, a myth. Great leaders build great teams. They listen. They include. They create cultures where people feel heard, valued, and motivated to contribute their best. They break down silos and foster cross-functional collaboration that leads to richer ideas and more creative solutions.

A business leader who embraces this farming spirit focuses especially on collective synergy. Like a cooperative of farmers sharing resources for the greater good, collaborative leaders create ecosystems of trust and mutual success.

Creative Cultivation: Problem-Solving in Real Time

Every farmer knows that something will go wrong. Maybe the tractor breaks. Maybe pests damage the crops. Maybe prices drop unexpectedly. Problem-solving is part of the daily rhythm—adapt, adjust, improvise, overcome.

The best leaders bring this same mindset to the boardroom. When sales drop or competition spikes, they do not panic, they get curious. They gather data, talk to customers, listen to their teams, and explore new possibilities. They treat problems not as roadblocks but as invitations to innovate.

One retail executive, faced with declining in-store traffic, did not cut costs reactively. Instead, she invited customers into the conversation. What did they want? What were they missing? That feedback sparked a transformation: new store layouts, community events, better digital integration. Sales returned—not through fear, but through thoughtful, collaborative problem-solving.

Stewardship Over Exploitation: Leading with Sustainability

Modern farmers understand that their work is not just about yield, it is about legacy. They care for the land so that it can care for future generations. This ethic of sustainability is increasingly mirrored in today's most effective business leaders.

Corporate social responsibility is no longer a niche, it is a necessity. Leaders who adopt ethical sourcing, reduce waste, and invest in community well-being are not only doing the right thing—they are earning the trust of employees and consumers alike. Transparency, accountability, and environmental awareness are no longer optional. They are strategic advantages.

A beverage company that partners with sustainable farms, shares its impact reports, and invests in the well-being of its suppliers is not just managing optics, it is building loyalty, attracting top talent, and securing a future where business and the planet can thrive together.

Counting the Costs: Financial Wisdom

Behind every successful farm is a farmer who knows the numbers, profit margins, input costs, debt cycles, weather insurance, financial literacy is non-negotiable. Good farmers track everything because their survival depends on it.

Business leaders need the same clarity. Cash flow, budgets, investments, and risk analysis form the roots of informed decisions. Financially wise leaders can spot trouble early, pivot when necessary, and invest confidently in growth. They know how to balance vision with practicality and ambition with sustainability.

At a startup, this may mean reworking a budget to extend runway without killing momentum. For a mid-sized business, it may mean reinvesting profits into employee development or product innovation. Whatever the context, financial acumen ensures that big dreams do not outrun the organization's ability to support them.

From Soil to Strategy: Leadership That Grows

Leadership, like farming, is not about force, it is about cultivation. It is about tending to people, ideas, and systems with care. It is about understanding the seasons, respecting the environment, and making choices that balance today's needs with tomorrow's potential.

When leaders adopt a farmer's mindset, they begin to see their teams not as units to manage, but as fields to grow. They recognize that every person, every challenge, every opportunity is part of a greater cycle.

With patience, vision, and stewardship, they can build something not only successful but enduring.

In the chapters ahead, we will continue exploring how purpose, presence, and principled action help leaders create cultures of meaning and momentum. For now, however, let us pause and remember: the strongest leaders are not those who demand growth; they are those who cultivate it.

Example: Community Leadership

In a small rural town, a farmer named John was renowned not just for his bountiful harvests, but also for his exceptional leadership skills. Understanding that farming is not just about individual success but community growth, John initiated a cooperative program among local farmers. He organized monthly meetings where farmers could share techniques, resources, and market insights. This collaboration not only increased crop yields but also fostered a sense of unity and support within the farming community, allowing them to tackle challenges such as fluctuating market prices and climate change together.

Recognizing the importance of sustainable practices, John took it upon himself to educate others about environmentally friendly farming methods. He hosted workshops on crop rotation, organic farming, and water conservation, inviting experts to share their knowledge. His leadership inspired many farmers to adopt these practices, leading to healthier soils and improved biodiversity in the area. By championing sustainability, John positioned his farm—and the community—at the forefront of modern agricultural practices, ensuring long-term viability and resilience against environmental challenges.

John's commitment to leadership extended beyond farming techniques. He actively engaged with local schools, introducing agricultural education programs that connected students with the farming process. By inviting children to participate in planting and harvesting, John instilled a sense of responsibility and awareness about food sources in the younger generation. His passion for farming and community development not only empowered his peers but also created a legacy that encouraged future farmers to lead with integrity and innovation. Through his efforts, John exemplified how effective leadership can cultivate both personal and communal growth in the agricultural sector.

Example: Business Leadership

In a rapidly evolving agricultural landscape, Farmer Sarah distinguished herself as a formidable business leader. By leveraging modern technology, she transformed her family farm into a thriving enterprise. Recognizing the potential of data analytics, Sarah invested in precision farming tools that monitor soil health and crop conditions. This strategic move allowed her to optimize resource use and maximize yields, significantly increasing her profitability. Her innovative approach not only improved her bottom line but also served as an inspiration for neighboring farmers, showcasing how embracing technology can enhance traditional farming practices.

Sarah's business acumen extended beyond operational efficiency; she also excelled in marketing her products. Understanding the growing consumer demand for organic produce, she launched a direct-to-consumer subscription service that connects her farm with local households. By utilizing social media and engaging in storytelling, Sarah built a strong brand identity that resonates with health-conscious consumers. This initiative not only provided her with a steady revenue stream but also fostered community ties, as customers felt more connected to the source of their food. Through her savvy marketing strategies, Sarah successfully carved out a niche in a competitive market.

Besides her entrepreneurial efforts, Sarah believes in the importance of mentorship and community involvement. She regularly hosts workshops for aspiring farmers, sharing insights on business planning and financial management. By offering her expertise, Sarah empowers others to pursue their agricultural ambitions, creating a network of support within the farming community. Her commitment to nurturing the next generation of farmers reflects her understanding that sustainable business leadership is about collaboration and knowledge-sharing. Through her multifaceted approach, Sarah exemplifies how a farmer can not only excel in business but also uplift an entire community, ensuring a prosperous future for all.

Harvesting Success

The skills developed through farming such as resilience, long-term planning, resource management, collaboration, problem-solving, sustainability, and financial acumen, offer invaluable lessons for business leadership. By embracing these principles, leaders can cultivate robust, adaptive organizations that thrive in the face of challenges.

As the business landscape continues to evolve, the integration of these farming skills into leadership practices may be the key to sustainable success. Just as a farmer tends to their crops with care and foresight, business leaders must approach their roles with a commitment to nurturing talent, fostering collaboration, and planning for the future.

Whether in the fields or the boardroom, the principles of effective management remain strikingly similar. By recognizing and applying the lessons learned from farming, leaders can sow the seeds for success and reap the rewards of a thriving organization.

As we shift from the fields to the front office, another unconventional source of leadership wisdom comes into view—not from soil and seasons, but from the dugouts and data sheets of professional baseball. *Moneyball*, both the bestselling book and the acclaimed film, tells the story of how the Oakland Athletics (A's) challenged long-held traditions and redefined success through bold thinking, analytical precision, and leadership that valued substance over style. In the next chapter, we explore how the lessons of *Moneyball*—questioning assumptions, embracing data-driven decisions, and leading with conviction—offer powerful insights for modern leaders looking to innovate, optimize, and win in today's competitive landscape.

Chapter 12

An Island of Misfit Toys: Leadership Lessons from "Moneyball"

"Of the twenty thousand knowable players for us to consider, I believe that there is a championship team of twenty five people that we can afford. Because everyone else in baseball undervalues them. Like an island of misfit toys."

– Peter Brand

Moneyball, both Michael Lewis's groundbreaking book and the acclaimed film adaptation, told the story of the Oakland Athletics and their revolutionary approach to baseball management. At its core, *Moneyball* is about challenging traditional paradigms, leveraging data, and recognizing potential where others see limitations. While the narrative revolves around sports, the lessons derived from it transcend the baseball diamond, offering profound insights into leadership applicable in any field.

What is Moneyball?

Moneyball is a revolutionary approach to baseball management that emerged during the early 2000s, centered on the Oakland Athletics (A's) and their general manager, Billy Beane. Faced with a tight budget, Beane recognized that traditional methods of scouting and player evaluation were insufficient for building a competitive team. Instead of relying on conventional metrics and subjective assessments, he turned to sabermetrics—an analytical approach that uses statistical data to assess player performance. This shift allowed the A's to identify undervalued players who could contribute significantly to the team's success without breaking the bank.

The collaboration between Beane and Peter Brand, a young Yale economics graduate, played a crucial role in this transformation. Brand introduced Beane to advanced statistical models that emphasized metrics like on-base percentage over traditional stats like batting average. By focusing on these overlooked aspects of player performance, the A's were able to assemble a roster filled with players others dismissed. This innovative strategy not only challenged the status quo in baseball but also demonstrated that a well-informed approach to player selection could yield remarkable results, even without the financial resources of larger teams.

The success of the A's in the 2002 season, where they achieved a record-breaking twenty-game winning streak, proved the effectiveness of the *Moneyball* philosophy. Despite facing skepticism from traditionalists, Beane's methods gained traction and eventually influenced the entire sport, leading to a greater acceptance of data analytics in baseball and beyond. *Moneyball* serves as a powerful reminder of how challenging established norms and embracing new ideas can lead to groundbreaking achievements, reshaping the way organizations approach problem-solving and decision-making in various fields.

Who is Billy Beane?

Billy Beane is a former professional baseball player and the current executive vice president of baseball operations for the Oakland Athletics. Born on March 29, 1962, in Orlando, Florida, Beane was a talented athlete who played college baseball at Stanford University. He was drafted by the New York Mets in 1980 and spent several years in the minor leagues before having a brief Major League Baseball (MLB) career. Despite his playing career not reaching the heights he had hoped for, Beane's understanding of the game and keen analytical mind set the stage for his future success in baseball management.

Beane is perhaps best known for his innovative approach to team building, which he famously applied while serving as general manager of the Oakland Athletics in the early 2000s. Faced with a limited budget compared to other teams, Beane adopted a data-driven strategy that emphasized advanced statistics and sabermetrics. This approach not only allowed the Athletics to compete effectively against wealthier teams but also revolutionized the way baseball organizations evaluate talent.

Beane's philosophy has had a lasting impact on the sport, influencing how many teams approach player evaluation and roster construction. His commitment to leveraging analytics continues to resonate throughout Major League Baseball, as organizations increasingly rely on data to inform decision-making. Through his innovative thinking and willingness to challenge traditional baseball norms, Billy Beane has solidified his legacy as a transformative figure in the world of sports management.

This chapter explores the key leadership lessons from Beane's management style as shown in *Moneyball*, illustrating how they can be applied in various organizational contexts to foster innovation, resilience, and long-term success.

Embracing Data-Driven Decision Making

One of the most significant contributions of *Moneyball* is its advocacy for data-driven decision-making. Billy Beane, who was the general manager of the Oakland Athletics, revolutionized the way teams evaluate talent by focusing on statistics and analytics rather than traditional scouting reports. He recognized that conventional wisdom often led to flawed assessments of player value.

Beane's approach exemplifies the power of analytics in making informed decisions. He utilized sabermetrics to identify undervalued players who could contribute to the team's success without the hefty price tag of star players. This method not only helped the A's compete with wealthier teams but also demonstrated the effectiveness of using data to challenge assumptions.

As a leader, embracing data is crucial. In today's fast-paced environment, relying solely on intuition can result in poor decisions. Leaders should cultivate a culture that prioritizes data, enabling teams to make evidence-based decisions. This involves investing in tools and training to help team members interpret data effectively and apply to their work.

Challenge the Status Quo

Billy Beane's journey was fraught with skepticism from traditionalists who doubted his unconventional methods. By challenging the status quo, he not only reshaped the A's but also sparked a broader conversation about how teams evaluate talent and build competitive rosters.

Beane's willingness to question established norms is a vital lesson for leaders: complacency stifles innovation. Organizations that rest on their laurels risk being outpaced by competitors who are more willing to adapt and evolve.

Leaders should encourage a culture of questioning and experimentation. This means creating an environment where team members feel safe to propose new ideas and challenge existing practices. By fostering open dialogue and being receptive to feedback, leaders can drive continuous improvement and innovation.

Foster a Culture of Collaboration

The success of the Oakland Athletics was a collective effort. Beane collaborated closely with the coaching staff to implement their new strategy. This collaboration was essential in integrating analytics into the team's operations and ensuring everyone was on board with the new vision.

Effective leadership is rooted in collaboration. Beane understood that individual brilliance is not enough; a cohesive team working toward a common goal is essential for success. By valuing diverse perspectives and encouraging teamwork, leaders can cultivate a sense of unity and shared purpose.

Leaders should actively promote collaboration within their teams. This can be achieved by establishing clear communication channels, encouraging cross-functional teams, and celebrating collective achievements. By creating a culture where everyone feels valued and heard, leaders can enhance team morale and productivity.

Value the Underdogs

Moneyball emphasizes the importance of recognizing potential in overlooked players. Peter Brand is quoted as comparing the roster they created to an 'Island of misfit toys.' Beane's strategy involved finding talent that others dismissed, demonstrating that value can often be found in unexpected places.

Leaders should be attuned to the unique strengths of their team members, even if they do not fit the conventional mold. By identifying and nurturing talent that may have been overlooked, organizations can unlock new levels of creativity and innovation.

Leaders can adopt a more inclusive approach to talent management. This involves creating pathways for individuals from diverse backgrounds and experiences to contribute to the organization. Investing in employee development and providing mentorship opportunities can help uncover hidden talents and foster a more dynamic workforce.

Focus on Long-Term Goals

Beane understood that building a competitive team was not just about immediate wins but rather about sustainable success. He made decisions that prioritized the long-term health of the organization, even if it meant sacrificing short-term gains.

Effective leaders maintain a clear vision for the future. By focusing on long-term goals, they can guide their teams through challenges and setbacks without losing sight of their ultimate objectives. This forward-thinking approach helps instill resilience and perseverance within the team.

Leaders should regularly communicate their vision and strategic goals to their teams. This involves setting measurable objectives and celebrating milestones along the way. By keeping everyone aligned with the long-term vision, leaders can foster a sense of purpose and direction.

Be Willing to Take Risks

Beane's approach to team-building involved significant risk. He opted for a strategy that defied traditional logic, particularly in how he structured the roster. His willingness to embrace uncertainty ultimately paid off, leading the A's to unprecedented success.

Leadership often involves making tough decisions and taking calculated risks. Beane's story illustrates that courage and conviction are essential traits for leaders who wish to drive innovation and change.

Leaders should cultivate a mindset of calculated risk-taking within their teams. This involves encouraging experimentation and learning from failures. By framing challenges as opportunities for growth, leaders can empower their teams to push boundaries and explore new avenues.

Adaptability is Key

As the landscape of baseball evolved, Beane continually adapted his strategies to stay relevant. He was not afraid to pivot when necessary, demonstrating the importance of flexibility in leadership.

In today's rapidly changing business environment, adaptability is more important than ever. Leaders must be prepared to respond to shifts in market dynamics, customer preferences, and technological advancements.

Leaders should foster a culture of agility within their organizations. This involves encouraging teams to stay informed about industry trends and be proactive in adapting to changes. By promoting a mindset of resilience and flexibility, leaders can better navigate uncertainty and capitalize on emerging opportunities.

Build Trust and Credibility

A vital aspect of Beane's leadership was the trust he built within his team. By standing firm in his beliefs and demonstrating the effectiveness of his approach, he gradually earned the respect of players, coaches, and management alike.

Trust is a cornerstone of effective leadership. When team members trust their leader, they are more likely to be engaged, motivated, and willing to take risks. Building trust requires transparency, integrity, and consistency in actions.

Leaders should prioritize building trust within their teams. This includes being open about decision-making processes, acknowledging mistakes, and following through on commitments. By fostering an environment of trust, leaders can enhance collaboration and commitment among team members.

Continuous Learning and Improvement

Moneyball underscores the importance of continuous learning. Beane and his team were always seeking new ways to improve, whether through refining their analytics or exploring new player acquisition strategies.

Adopting a growth mindset is essential for leaders who wish to inspire their teams. This mindset encourages individuals to view challenges as opportunities for learning and development.

Leaders should promote a culture of continuous learning within their organizations. This can be achieved by providing access to training resources, encouraging professional development, and facilitating knowledge sharing among team members. By fostering a culture of curiosity and improvement, leaders can drive innovation and adaptability.

Ultimately, *Moneyball* is not just a story about baseball; it is a masterclass in business leadership that highlights the significance of adaptability, analytical thinking, and team dynamics. Beane's journey illustrates how effective leaders can harness data and technology to drive performance, challenge preconceived notions, and build resilient organizations. In an ever-evolving marketplace, the principles derived from Beane's experience resonate deeply, reinforcing the idea that true leadership involves not only strategic foresight but also the ability to cultivate a culture of innovation and collaboration.

As the business landscape continues to evolve, so too must the environments in which leadership is practiced. Just as Beane embraced unconventional methods to transform a traditional institution, today's leaders are increasingly called upon to reimagine how teams operate and thrive outside conventional office spaces. The rise of remote work has presented both a challenge and an opportunity, demanding the same adaptability, analytical thinking, and cultural intentionality that defined Beane's success. In the next chapter, we will explore what it means to lead effectively in this new frontier, where trust, communication, and digital fluency are the cornerstones of high-performing, distributed teams.

Chapter 13

'You are on Mute': Leading in the Modern Remote Work Environment

"In the world of remote work, the key is not to prioritize what's on your schedule, but to schedule your priorities."

– Stephen Covey

The landscape of work has undergone a seismic shift in recent years, particularly with the rise of remote work. As organizations adapt to this new normal, leadership styles must also evolve to meet the unique challenges and opportunities presented by remote environments. One approach that has gained significant traction is servant leadership—a philosophy that prioritizes the growth and well-being of team members. This chapter explores what servant leadership looks like in a modern remote work environment, examining its principles, practices, and real-world applications.

Understanding Servant Leadership

Servant leadership is a leadership philosophy that prioritizes the growth and well-being of individuals and communities over the traditional notion of hierarchical power and authority. Coined by Robert K. Greenleaf in the 1970s, the concept emphasizes that effective leaders serve their teams by placing their needs first and empowering them to develop their skills and potential. At its core, servant leadership is about fostering a collaborative environment where leaders actively listen, empathize, and support their team members, creating a culture of trust and mutual respect. This approach challenges conventional leadership models by focusing on service rather than control, encouraging leaders to adopt a more humble and supportive role.

One of the key principles of servant leadership is the emphasis on empathy and understanding. Servant leaders strive to connect with their team members on a personal level, recognizing the unique challenges and experiences each individual may face. By actively listening and validating employees' feelings, servant leaders create a safe space where team members can express their thoughts and concerns openly. This empathetic approach fosters strong relationships, enhances team cohesion, and cultivates a positive work environment, ultimately driving higher engagement and productivity. In this way, servant leadership not only benefits individual team members but also strengthens the overall effectiveness of the organization.

Another essential aspect of servant leadership is the commitment to the development of others. Servant leaders prioritize the growth of their team members by providing opportunities for learning, skill-building, and career advancement. This focus on personal and professional development not only empowers employees but also contributes to a more capable and innovative workforce. By investing in their team's growth, servant leaders create a culture of continuous improvement, thereby encouraging individuals to take risks, share ideas, and contribute to the organization's mission. Ultimately, servant leadership fosters a sense of community and shared purpose, enabling organizations to thrive and adapt in an ever-changing landscape.

The importance of Servant Leadership in Remote Work

Adapting to Isolation

Remote work can lead to feelings of isolation and disconnection among team members. Servant leaders must recognize and address the unique emotional and psychological challenges that team members face when working apart from one another. Isolation can lead to feelings of loneliness, decreased motivation, and diminished collaboration, ultimately affecting productivity and job satisfaction. Servant leaders who actively seek to understand these challenges can foster a supportive environment by implementing strategies that promote connection, such as regular check-ins, virtual team-building activities, and open forums for sharing experiences.

By adapting their leadership style to prioritize the well-being and engagement of their team members, servant leaders can create a sense of community and belonging, ensuring that employees remain connected and motivated despite the physical distance. This adaptability not only strengthens individual resilience but also enhances overall team cohesion, driving collective success in remote settings.

Enhancing Engagement

High levels of engagement directly correlate with employee satisfaction, productivity, and retention. In a virtual environment where employees are more likely to feel disconnected from their colleagues and the organization's mission, servant leaders must actively cultivate a sense of involvement, accountability and commitment among team members. By fostering open communication, recognizing achievements, and providing opportunities for professional development, leaders can create an environment where employees feel valued and motivated to contribute their best efforts. Engaged employees are more likely to collaborate effectively, share innovative ideas, and remain loyal to the organization, ultimately driving collective success. Servant leaders who prioritize engagement not only enhance individual performance but also strengthen the overall health of the remote team, ensuring a thriving and cohesive work culture.

Promoting Well-Being

An employee's mental and physical health directly impacts their performance and overall job satisfaction. In a virtual environment where isolation and stress may heighten, servant leaders must create a supportive atmosphere that prioritizes employee well-being. By actively encouraging work-life balance, offering resources for mental health support, and fostering open dialogue about challenges, leaders show their commitment to the holistic health of their team members. This focus on well-being not only helps to reduce burnout and absenteeism, but also cultivates a more engaged and resilient workforce. When employees feel cared for and supported, they are more likely to be productive, creative, and committed to their work, ultimately driving the organization's success and fostering a positive, collaborative culture.

Fostering Innovation

Remote work requires new ways of thinking and problem-solving. Fostering innovation enables teams to adapt, evolve, and remain competitive in a rapidly changing business landscape. In a virtual environment, traditional brainstorming sessions and spontaneous idea exchanges are limited; therefore, servant leaders must create an atmosphere that promotes creativity and experimentation. By promoting a culture of psychological safety, where team members feel comfortable sharing their ideas without fear of judgment, leaders can inspire collaboration and diverse thinking. Providing resources and opportunities for skill development empowers employees to explore new solutions and approaches. When servant leaders prioritize innovation, they not only enhance problem-solving capabilities but also boost employee engagement and satisfaction, as team members feel their contributions are valued and impactful. Ultimately, fostering innovation helps organizations thrive, driving growth and adaptability in an increasingly dynamic remote work setting.

Key Characteristics of Servant Leadership in Remote Contexts

Empathy and Active Listening

Effective servant leaders demonstrate empathy by genuinely understanding the feelings and perspectives of their team members. Empathy fosters a sense of belonging and trust among team members. In a virtual environment where non-verbal cues are often lost, empathy can help leaders recognize the challenges their employees face, whether related to work-life balance, mental health, or communication barriers. This understanding enables leaders to respond effectively, supportively, and with compassion, creating a more inclusive and motivated workforce.

Active listening complements empathy by ensuring that leaders fully engage with their team members' concerns and ideas. In remote settings, where communication can be easily misinterpreted or overlooked, active listening helps to validate employees' experiences and perspectives. By listening attentively and responding thoughtfully, servant leaders make team members feel valued and encouraged to share their thoughts. This two-way communication not only enhances collaboration and problem-solving but also reinforces a culture of openness and support—vital traits for boosting morale and productivity in a distributed team.

Open Communication

The physical separation of remote work can lead to misunderstandings and feelings of isolation. When leaders prioritize transparent communication, they create a culture of trust and safety that encourages team members to express their thoughts and concerns freely. This openness enables leaders to address issues proactively, ensuring that employees feel heard and valued.

As informal interactions are limited in a virtual setting, creating open lines of communication can help maintain strong relationships and promote a cohesive team dynamic, ultimately enhancing collaboration and productivity.

Open communication in a remote work setting facilitates alignment and clarity around goals, expectations, and responsibilities. Servant leaders who communicate openly can provide regular updates, share feedback, and solicit input from their team members, which helps to keep everyone on the same page. This clarity not only minimizes miscommunication but also empowers employees by involving them in decision-making processes. Team members who feel informed are more likely to take ownership of their roles and contribute to the organization's success. Thus, open communication is not just a tool for effective management; it is a foundational element that supports the servant leadership ethos of prioritizing the needs and growth of team members.

Support and Development

In a virtual environment, the lack of face-to-face interaction can lead to feelings of isolation and disconnection. Servant leaders who prioritize support create an atmosphere where team members feel valued and understood. By actively offering assistance, whether through regular check-ins, mentorship, or resources for professional growth, leaders demonstrate their commitment to the well-being and success of their employees. This support not only fosters resilience during uncertainty, but also nurtures a sense of community amongst team members.

Prioritizing employee development is essential for nurturing talent and enhancing team performance, even in a remote setting. Servant leaders who provide training opportunities, skill development, and career advancement pathways help their employees realize their potential and contribute more effectively to the organization. This commitment to development builds a culture of continuous learning. In a remote work context, where individuals may have varied experiences and skill sets, tailored development initiatives can bridge gaps and promote collaboration. Ultimately, by emphasizing support and development, servant leaders empower their team members and drive organizational success by fostering a skilled, motivated, and cohesive workforce.

Autonomy and Empowerment

Servant leaders empower their team members by delegating responsibilities and allowing them to make decisions. By granting team members the freedom to make decisions about their work, servant leaders foster a sense of ownership and accountability. This autonomy encourages employees to take initiative, be creative, and develop solutions that align with their unique strengths and perspectives. In remote settings where direct supervision is limited, empowering individuals to trust their judgment enhances their confidence and also leads to increased job satisfaction and motivation. When team members feel they have control over their work, they are more likely to be engaged and committed to achieving organizational goals.

Empowerment also plays a crucial role in promoting collaboration and innovation within remote teams. Servant leaders who actively encourage their employees to share ideas and take part in decision-making processes create a culture of inclusivity and respect. This collaborative approach allows diverse perspectives to be heard and valued, leading to more comprehensive solutions and fostering a sense of community, even at a distance.

When employees feel empowered, they are more likely to support one another and contribute to a positive team dynamic. By prioritizing autonomy and empowerment, servant leaders cultivate an environment where team members can thrive, fueling both individual growth and organizational success in a remote work setting.

Recognizing Achievements

In a remote environment, recognition is often overlooked, leaving employees feeling isolated and disconnected from their contributions to the organization's success. By actively acknowledging individual and team accomplishments, servant leaders reinforce the value of each team member's efforts, fostering a sense of belonging and appreciation. This recognition not only boosts morale but also motivates employees to continue performing at their best, knowing that their hard work is seen and valued. When leaders take the time to celebrate achievements, they enhance overall job satisfaction and strengthen the emotional connection employees feel toward their organization.

Recognizing achievements in a remote setting contributes to a culture of transparency and trust. When servant leaders publicly celebrate successes, whether through virtual shout-outs, recognition in meetings, or acknowledgement in team communications platforms, they create an environment where everyone feels encouraged to strive for excellence. This practice not only highlights individual contributions but also promotes teamwork and collaboration, as employees are inspired by one another's successes. Such recognition can spark healthy competition and a shared commitment to achieving collective goals. By prioritizing the recognition of employee achievements, servant leaders cultivate an engaged, motivated, and cohesive remote workforce that is aligned with the organization's mission and values.

Flexibility and Understanding

Remote work often requires flexibility due to varying personal and professional circumstances such as work-life balance and time zone differences. It can blur the boundaries between professional and personal life, leading to stress and burnout if not managed effectively. Servant leaders who show flexibility in their approach–such as accommodating varied work hours or allowing for personal commitments–show that they value their employees' well-being. This adaptability fosters a supportive environment where team members feel empowered to manage their responsibilities effectively, leading to increased productivity and job satisfaction.

Understanding is important in cultivating a compassionate leadership style that resonates with remote teams. By taking the time to listen to employees' concerns and perspectives, servant leaders can better grasp the nuances of their experiences. This understanding enables leaders to act with empathy, tailoring their support to meet individual needs. When employees feel that their circumstances are recognized and considered, it strengthens their trust in leadership and enhances their commitment to the organization. Together, flexibility and understanding create a culture of respect and collaboration, where team members are more likely to engage openly, share challenges, and seek help when needed. This supportive atmosphere ultimately contributes to a resilient and high-performing remote workforce.

Building a Sense of Community

Creating a cohesive team culture is essential in remote settings. Servant leaders who prioritize community foster an environment where team members feel a sense of belonging, which is essential for maintaining morale and engagement. By facilitating opportunities for social interaction–such as virtual team-building activities, informal check-ins, or collaborative projects–leaders can help create bonds among employees. This sense of community not only enhances overall job satisfaction but also encourages individuals to support one another, share ideas, and work together toward common goals.

A strong sense of community promotes a culture of trust and collaboration, which is vital for effective teamwork in a remote setting. When employees feel connected to their peers, they are more likely to share their thoughts and contribute actively to discussions, leading to innovative solutions and improved problem-solving. Servant leaders who emphasize community-building demonstrate their commitment to the holistic well-being of their team, which can lead to increased loyalty and retention. A united team can navigate challenges more effectively, as members feel comfortable reaching out for support and collaborating on solutions. Ultimately, a sense of community enhances individual employee experiences while also driving collective success.

Vision and Purpose

Servant leaders articulate a clear vision and purpose for the team, especially in a remote setting where employees may lack the daily interactions that reinforce organizational goals. A well-articulated vision provides a roadmap for both leaders and team members, helping to align efforts and maintain focus on shared objectives. In a virtual environment, where distractions may abound and team members operate independently, a strong sense of purpose can keep employees engaged and committed. Servant leaders who communicate a compelling vision not only inspire their teams, but also empower them to take ownership of their roles and contributions, fostering a collective commitment to achieving the organization's goals.

A defined vision and purpose serve as guiding principles during challenging times, helping teams navigate uncertainty and change. In remote work settings, where adaptability is often required, having a clear direction allows teams to pivot effectively while remaining aligned with overarching objectives. Servant leaders who embody and communicate their vision reinforce a culture of resilience and innovation. Ultimately, a strong vision and purpose not only unify remote teams, but also cultivate a sense of belonging and fulfillment, both of which are vital for sustained engagement and success.

Practical Applications of Servant Leadership

To illustrate how servant leadership can be effectively implemented in a remote work environment, consider the following practical applications:

Regular One-on-One Meetings

Scheduled biweekly or monthly one-on-one meetings are crucial, as they foster open communication and trust between leaders and their team members. These meetings provide a dedicated space for leaders to listen actively to the concerns, ideas, and feedback of their employees. By prioritizing these interactions, servant leaders show their commitment to understanding each team member's needs and challenges, which in turn cultivates a supportive environment. This ongoing dialogue not only helps identify and address issues early, but also empowers employees by making them feel valued and heard, reinforcing their sense of belonging within the organization.

One-on-one meetings serve as an essential tool for personal and professional development. Servant leaders can use this time to mentor and coach their team members, helping them set goals and navigate their career paths. By focusing on the growth and well-being of each individual, leaders can align their team members' personal aspirations with organizational objectives, creating a more engaged and motivated workforce. These meetings also allow for the recognition of achievements and progress, which boosts morale and encourages continuous improvement. Ultimately, regular one-on-ones are a foundational practice in servant leadership that strengthens relationships, enhances team dynamics, and drives overall organizational success.

Virtual Open-Door Policy

Maintaining a virtual open-door policy is vital as it encourages transparency and accessibility in a remote work environment. This approach allows team members to feel comfortable reaching out to their leaders without the barriers that can often arise in traditional hierarchical structures. By fostering an atmosphere where employees can share their thoughts, concerns, and ideas freely, servant leaders demonstrate their commitment to being approachable and supportive. This accessibility not only builds trust but also empowers team members to voice their opinions and contribute to decision-making processes, ultimately enhancing collaboration and innovation.

A virtual open-door policy reinforces the importance of effective communication and connection in a remote setting. Servant leaders who embrace this practice stay attuned to the needs and challenges of their team, even when they are not physically present. Regular check-ins and an open invitation for dialogue help leaders identify potential issues early and provide the necessary support to their team members. By prioritizing open communication, servant leaders can nurture a culture of inclusivity and belonging, where employees feel valued and engaged. This, in turn, leads to higher morale and productivity, creating a more resilient and cohesive team, regardless of geographical barriers.

Feedback Loops

Implementing regular feedback loops creates a continuous cycle of communication that fosters growth and development. By actively seeking and providing feedback, servant leaders demonstrate their commitment to the personal and professional advancement of their team members. This practice encourages an environment in which employees feel safe to express their ideas, concerns, and suggestions, knowing that their input is valued. Feedback loops not only help identify areas for improvement but also celebrate successes, reinforcing positive behaviors and motivating team members to strive for excellence.

Feedback loops also enhance the overall effectiveness of a team by promoting a culture of accountability and responsiveness. Servant leaders who prioritize these loops can quickly adapt their strategies based on the insights they gather from their team. This responsiveness not only enhances decision-making but also ensures that team members feel their contributions have a direct impact on the organization's success. By fostering an atmosphere of open dialogue and mutual respect, feedback loops empower employees to take ownership of their roles and collaborate more effectively, ultimately leading to improved performance and a stronger, more cohesive team dynamic.

Professional Development Plans

Work with each team member to create personalized development plans that align individual growth with organizational goals, fostering a culture of continuous improvement. By actively engaging in the development of their team members, servant leaders demonstrate their commitment to nurturing talent and fostering a sense of purpose within the organization. These plans provide clear pathways for employees to enhance their skills, pursue new opportunities, and achieve their career aspirations. When team members see that their leaders are invested in their growth, it cultivates a sense of loyalty and motivation, ultimately driving higher levels of engagement and performance.

Professional development plans also encourage accountability and support within the team. Servant leaders can use these plans to facilitate regular check-ins and discussions about progress, challenges, and future goals. This ongoing dialogue not only helps individuals stay focused on their development objectives but also allows leaders to tailor their support and resources to meet each employee's unique needs. By prioritizing professional development, servant leaders create an environment where learning is valued and encouraged, leading to a more skilled and adaptable workforce. This commitment to growth not only benefits individual employees but also strengthens the organization as a whole, fostering innovation and resilience in a rapidly changing business landscape.

Recognition Programs

Establish a recognition program that highlights individual and team achievements. This can include monthly awards, shout-outs during team meetings, or a dedicated channel for sharing accomplishments. Recognition programs reinforce a culture of appreciation and value within an organization. By acknowledging the contributions and achievements of team members, servant leaders demonstrate their commitment to recognizing individual efforts and fostering a sense of belonging. These programs not only boost employee morale but also enhance motivation, as individuals are more likely to feel inspired to perform at their best when their hard work is celebrated. This positive reinforcement creates an environment where employees feel seen and valued, leading to increased engagement and loyalty to the organization.

Recognition programs also foster collaboration and a sense of community among team members. When leaders publicly celebrate achievements, it encourages others to recognize one another's efforts as well, promoting a culture of mutual support and teamwork. This collaborative spirit aligns with the principles of servant leadership, where the focus is on serving others and lifting them up. By creating a framework for recognizing contributions, servant leaders can cultivate a more cohesive team dynamic, ultimately driving better performance and innovation. In this way, recognition programs not only enhance individual satisfaction but also contribute to the overall success and health of the organization.

Encourage Social Interaction

As a servant leader, encouraging social interaction, especially for a virtual workforce, is crucial. Social interactions foster a sense of community and belonging among team members. In a remote setting, employees can often feel isolated, which can lead to disengagement and reduced morale. By promoting regular social interactions through virtual team-building activities, informal coffee chats, or collaborative projects, servant leaders help create connections that transcend job titles and roles. This sense of camaraderie enables team members to build trust and rapport, making them more comfortable sharing ideas and collaborating effectively. When employees feel connected, they are more likely to be engaged, motivated, and committed to their team's success.

Encouraging social interaction aligns with the principles of servant leadership by prioritizing the well-being and development of individuals. When leaders foster an environment where socialization is valued, they demonstrate their commitment to the holistic growth of their team members. Informal interactions provide opportunities for employees to share personal experiences, exchange knowledge, and offer support to one another, all of which contribute to a positive workplace culture. This not only strengthens interpersonal relationships but also enhances overall team dynamics, leading to improved communication and collaboration. By emphasizing social interaction, servant leaders can ensure that their virtual teams remain cohesive, resilient, and aligned with their shared goals, ultimately driving better performance and job satisfaction.

Promoting Work-Life Balance

Encouraging team members to set boundaries by advocating for their time off and respecting personal commitments shows a leader's genuine concern for the well-being of their team members. When leaders prioritize the balance between professional responsibilities and personal life, they create an environment where employees feel supported and valued. This commitment helps to reduce stress and prevent burnout, which are common challenges in today's fast-paced work culture. Servant leaders who encourage flexible work arrangements and respect personal time signal that they care about their team's holistic welfare. This fosters a culture of trust and loyalty, as employees are more likely to feel engaged and productive when they know their leaders prioritize their health and happiness.

A strong emphasis on work-life balance also enhances overall organizational performance. When employees maintain a healthy balance, they tend to exhibit higher levels of job satisfaction and motivation, leading to increased productivity and creativity. Servant leaders can leverage this by encouraging their teams to pursue hobbies, spend time with family, and engage in self-care, which ultimately enhances their focus and effectiveness at work. By advocating for work-life balance, servant leaders not only contribute to the personal fulfillment of their employees, but also cultivate a more resilient and innovative workforce. This holistic approach aligns with the core values of servant leadership, reinforcing the idea that supporting others is essential for achieving collective success.

Utilize Technology

Leveraging technology facilitates effective communication and collaboration across diverse work environments. In a hybrid setup, where team members may work both remotely and in the office, tools such as videoconferencing, instant messaging, and collaborative platforms help bridge the gap between locations. Servant leaders can leverage these tools to maintain open lines of communication, ensuring that all employees feel included and informed, regardless of their work setting. This commitment to connectivity not only strengthens relationships but also allows leaders to remain attuned to the needs and challenges of their team members, reinforcing a culture of support and engagement.

Technology also empowers servant leaders to promote transparency and gather valuable feedback from their teams. Tools for project management, employee surveys, and performance tracking enable leaders to monitor progress and identify areas where additional support may be needed. By utilizing these technologies, servant leaders can act swiftly to address concerns based on real-time insights. This responsiveness fosters a sense of inclusivity and encourages team members to share their perspectives.

Ultimately, embracing technology not only enhances operational efficiency but also aligns with the servant leadership philosophy of prioritizing the growth and well-being of others, creating a more cohesive and motivated hybrid workforce.

Challenges of Servant Leadership in Remote Work

While servant leadership offers a variety of benefits, it also presents challenges, particularly in a remote context:

Maintaining Connection

Building relationships can be more challenging when team members do not meet face-to-face, often leading to feelings of isolation and disconnection. Without the spontaneous interactions that occur in a traditional office setting, employees may miss out on essential social bonds and informal communication that foster teamwork and camaraderie. Virtual communication tools can sometimes feel impersonal, making it difficult to build rapport and trust among colleagues. In addition, varying time zones and work schedules can hinder real-time collaboration, further complicating efforts to maintain a cohesive team environment. These factors may lead to misunderstandings, decreased morale, and a sense of detachment. Therefore, it's imperative for leaders to be intentional about creating opportunities for connection and engagement in remote work settings.

Overcoming Communication Barriers

Our reliance on digital tools may hinder the ability to have effective interactions. In a virtual environment, nuances such as tone, body language, and immediate feedback are often lost, leading to misunderstandings and misinterpretations. Varying levels of technological proficiency among team members can create disparities in communication effectiveness, further complicating collaboration. Time zone differences may also result in delayed responses, making it difficult to maintain a fluid conversation and address issues promptly. These barriers can contribute to a sense of disconnection and frustration, underscoring the need for leaders to implement clear communication strategies and foster an environment where open dialogue is encouraged and facilitated.

Balancing Support and Accountability

While providing support is essential, servant leaders must also hold team members accountable for their responsibilities. In a virtual environment, leaders may feel the need to offer extra support to combat feelings of isolation and uncertainty among employees, which can sometimes lead to a perception of leniency or a lack of structure. Conversely, ensuring accountability can be difficult, as monitoring performance is less straightforward without in-person oversight. This dynamic can create tension: employees may struggle with self-management while seeking support, and leaders may grapple with defining clear expectations without micromanaging. Achieving this balance is crucial to fostering a productive and motivated remote team, as it encourages independence while also providing the necessary resources for success.

Cultural Differences

In global remote teams, cultural differences can impact communication styles, work habits, and team dynamics. In a virtual environment, leaders must navigate varying perspectives on hierarchy, collaboration, and feedback, which may lead to misunderstandings or conflicts if not addressed properly. For example, employees from collectivist cultures might prioritize group harmony and consensus, while those from individualistic cultures may focus on personal achievements and assertiveness. Such differences can complicate collaboration and require leaders to be particularly sensitive and adaptive to their approach to foster inclusivity. A lack of shared cultural references can also hinder relationship-building and trust among team members, making it essential for leaders to cultivate cultural awareness and promote open dialogue to bridge these gaps effectively.

Servant leadership is a powerful approach that can significantly enhance the effectiveness of remote teams. By prioritizing the well-being and growth of team members, servant leaders create an engaging, supportive, and innovative work environment. As organizations continue to adapt to the challenges of remote work, embracing servant leadership principles will be crucial for fostering strong relationships, enhancing collaboration, and driving team success.

In this evolving landscape, leaders who embody the principles of servant leadership will not only navigate the complexities of remote work successfully but also inspire their teams to thrive, ensuring sustained organizational success in a changing world.

While servant leadership lays the foundation for strong internal team dynamics—especially in remote settings—no organization operates in a vacuum. The ability to build and maintain meaningful external relationships is equally vital to long-term success. Whether with partners, vendors, community stakeholders, or customers, these relationships extend a company's capacity for innovation, resilience, and impact. In the next chapter, we will examine how cultivating strategic external connections can amplify organizational effectiveness and create lasting value beyond the workplace.

Chapter 14

It's All About Relationships: The Value of External Business Relationships

"You can make more friends in two months by becoming interested in other people than you can in two years by trying to get other people interested in you."

– Dale Carnegie

In today's interconnected world, the success of any business is increasingly tied to its ability to cultivate and maintain relationships with external stakeholders. These stakeholders–ranging from customers and suppliers to investors, community members, and regulatory bodies–play a crucial role in shaping a company's trajectory. This chapter explores the various dimensions of business relationships with external stakeholders, emphasizing their value in enhancing reputation, driving innovation, and ensuring long-term sustainability.

Understanding External Stakeholders

External stakeholders are individuals or groups outside of a business that are affected by its operations. Their interests may vary widely, but their influence on a company's success is undeniable. Key categories of external stakeholders include:

Customers

The lifeblood of any organization is its customers. Their purchasing decisions and preferences shape product development, marketing strategies, and overall business operations. By understanding customer needs and feedback, business leaders can tailor their offerings to meet market demands, ensuring customer satisfaction and loyalty. This relationship not only drives sales but also fosters brand advocacy, as satisfied customers are more likely to recommend products and services to others, enhancing the company's reputation and market reach.

Customers play a crucial role in the competitive landscape. In today's digital age, consumers are empowered with access to vast amounts of information and alternatives, making their satisfaction and engagement paramount for a business's sustainability. Business leaders must prioritize customer relationships to cultivate trust and ensure long-term success. By actively listening to their customers, companies can innovate and adapt to changing market trends, thereby positioning themselves ahead of competitors. Customers are not just buyers; they are key partners in a business's journey toward achieving its strategic objectives.

Suppliers

These partners provide the necessary materials, products, and services that enable a company to operate effectively. A reliable supply chain is crucial for maintaining production schedules, ensuring quality, and managing costs. Business leaders demand from suppliers not only timely delivery of goods but also innovation and support in developing new products. Strong relationships with suppliers can lead to favorable terms, better pricing, and access to unique resources, all of which contribute to a company's competitive advantage.

Suppliers can significantly impact a company's reputation and sustainability practices. As consumers become increasingly aware of ethical sourcing and environmental impact, businesses must collaborate closely with suppliers who align with their values and standards. By working with responsible suppliers, business leaders can enhance their brand image and meet customer expectations regarding corporate social responsibility. Effective supplier management not only mitigates risks associated with supply chain disruptions but also fosters collaboration that can lead to joint innovation and long-term growth, making suppliers a critical component of a successful business strategy.

Investors

Shareholders and potential investors are crucial for securing capital that fuels growth and innovation within a company. By investing in a business, they enable leaders to fund new projects, expand operations, and explore new markets. This financial support is essential for executing strategic initiatives that can enhance profitability and long-term sustainability. In addition, investors often bring valuable expertise and networks that can guide business decisions, making their involvement not just about funding but also about strategic partnership.

Investors play a significant role in shaping a company's governance and accountability. Concerned with the overall performance and direction of the business, they encourage leaders to prioritize transparency, ethical practices, and sound financial management. This oversight helps mitigate risks and ensures that the company remains focused on delivering value not only to shareholders, including employees and customers. As a result, maintaining strong relationships with investors is vital for business leaders, as it fosters trust and confidence in the company's vision and strategy, ultimately driving long-term success.

Community Members

Businesses do not exist in isolation; they are part of a larger ecosystem that includes local residents, organizations, and institutions. Positive relationships with community members can enhance a company's image, foster goodwill, and encourage local support for its initiatives. When businesses engage with their communities through corporate social responsibility (CSR) programs, sponsorships, or local partnerships, they demonstrate a commitment to social values, which can lead to increased customer loyalty and brand advocacy.

Community members can provide valuable insights and feedback that help shape a business's operations and offerings. Understanding the unique needs and concerns of the local population allows business leaders to tailor their products and services to better serve the community. This proactive approach not only addresses potential issues before they escalate but also fosters a sense of belonging and collaboration between the company and its surroundings. In an age where consumers prioritize socially responsible and community-focused businesses, engaging with community members is essential for long-term success and sustainability. By nurturing these relationships, business leaders can create a positive impact that benefits both the community and the organization.

Regulatory Bodies

Compliance with laws and regulations is non-negotiable, and regulatory bodies establish the legal framework within which companies operate. These organizations set standards and guidelines that ensure compliance with laws related to health, safety, environmental impact, and fair competition. Business leaders must navigate these regulations to avoid legal penalties and maintain their licenses to operate. Understanding regulatory requirements helps companies mitigate risks and ensures that they adhere to best practices, thereby fostering a culture of accountability and ethical behavior. By engaging proactively with regulatory bodies, businesses can also influence policy development, advocating for regulations that support their industry while ensuring public interests are safeguarded.

Regulatory bodies can also drive innovation and improve operational efficiency by encouraging businesses to adopt new practices and technologies that comply with evolving regulations. For instance, environmental regulations may prompt companies to invest in sustainable practices, leading to cost savings and enhanced brand reputation. These bodies often provide resources and guidance to help businesses understand and implement compliance measures effectively. Such collaboration fosters an environment where businesses and regulators work together to achieve common goals, such as promoting fair competition and protecting consumer rights. For business leaders, maintaining positive interactions with regulatory bodies is essential not only for compliance but also for positioning their organizations favorably within a dynamic regulatory landscape.

Effective Engagement Strategies

Engagement strategies are crucial when working with external partners because they foster trust, collaboration, and mutual understanding. By actively communicating and involving stakeholders such as suppliers, customers, investors, and community members, business leaders can gather valuable insights and feedback that inform decision-making and strategy development. Engaging stakeholders helps to align their interests with the company's goals, reducing the likelihood of conflicts and enhancing overall satisfaction. Strong engagement can lead to long-term relationships that benefit both parties, creating a supportive network that drives innovation and resilience. In an increasingly interconnected world, effective stakeholder engagement not only enhances a company's reputation but also contributes to sustainable business practices and community well-being. Effective strategies include:

Enhancing Reputation and Credibility

One of the most significant advantages of nurturing relationships with external stakeholders is that it enhances a company's reputation and credibility. When a company is perceived as credible, stakeholders such as customers, investors, and suppliers are more likely to engage positively with the business. This trust leads to increased customer loyalty, repeat business, and positive word-of-mouth, which can significantly impact a company's bottom line. A solid reputation can attract new investors and partners who are looking for reliable and ethical organizations to collaborate with, ultimately contributing to the company's growth and sustainability.

A strong reputation acts as a buffer during times of crisis or controversy. Businesses that have established credibility are better positioned to navigate challenges, as stakeholders are more likely to support them when they trust the company's leadership and values. Engaging transparently with stakeholders and actively addressing their concerns can further reinforce this credibility, demonstrating that the company values their input and is committed to ethical practices. In today's competitive landscape, where information spreads rapidly through social media and online platforms, maintaining a positive reputation is not just beneficial but essential for long-term success. By prioritizing reputation and credibility in their engagement strategies, business leaders can build resilient relationships that support their overall business objectives.

Building Trust

Trust encourages open communication, allowing stakeholders to voice their concerns, provide feedback, and share insights. When stakeholders feel valued and heard, they are more likely to support the business, which can lead to enhanced loyalty and commitment. A trustworthy reputation helps mitigate potential conflicts and fosters a cooperative environment, enabling businesses to work together with their stakeholders toward common goals, thereby driving innovation and growth.

Trust serves as a shield during challenging times. Businesses that have cultivated strong, trusting relationships with their stakeholders are more likely to receive understanding and support when faced with issues such as crises, product recalls, or public relations challenges. Stakeholders are inclined to maintain their loyalty to a business they trust, viewing it as a reliable partner committed to ethical practices and transparency. This resilience is crucial in maintaining stability and sustaining operations in a competitive market.

Therefore, prioritizing trust-building in stakeholder engagement strategies not only enhances a company's reputation but also fosters long-term success, enabling business leaders to navigate complexities with greater confidence and support.

Reputation Management

A single negative incident can tarnish a company's reputation. In contrast, a positive reputation enhances stakeholder trust and loyalty, which can lead to increased customer retention, stronger investor interest, and better relationships with suppliers and community members. In today's digital age, where information spreads rapidly through social media and other online platforms, managing a company's reputation is more critical than ever. Proactively addressing potential issues, responding to stakeholder concerns, and showcasing positive achievements can help cultivate a favorable image that sets the business apart from competitors, ultimately driving growth and profitability.

Effective reputation management enables businesses to mitigate risks associated with negative publicity or crises. When a company has a strong reputation, it is more likely to weather storms, as stakeholders are inclined to give the business the benefit of the doubt. Transparent communication, consistent messaging, and active engagement with external stakeholders can help businesses navigate challenges better, preserving trust and minimizing damage.

A well-managed reputation attracts new opportunities such as partnerships and collaborations, as other organizations seek to align with reputable brands. Therefore, reputation management is not just about maintaining a positive image; it is a strategic approach that enhances stakeholder relationships and supports long-term business success.

Driving Innovation and Competitive Advantage

External stakeholders can be a rich source of innovative ideas and insights. Engaging with customers, suppliers, and industry experts allows businesses to tap into diverse perspectives and insights that can inspire new product development, enhance existing services, and streamline operations. By actively involving these stakeholders in the innovation process, leaders can better understand market needs and trends, ensuring that their offerings remain relevant and appealing. This collaborative approach not only accelerates innovation, but also makes stakeholders feel valued and invested in the company's success.

Leveraging external stakeholder engagement to drive innovation helps businesses differentiate themselves in competitive markets. In an era where consumers are increasingly looking for unique and customized solutions, companies that prioritize stakeholder input can quickly adapt to changing demands and preferences. This ability not only enhances customer satisfaction but also positions the business as a leader within its industry. A reputation for innovation can attract investors and partners eager to associate with forward-thinking organizations. By making stakeholder engagement a cornerstone of their innovation strategy, business leaders can build a sustainable competitive advantage that drives growth, and secures long-term viability in an ever-evolving marketplace.

Customer Insights

Customers are often the best sources of information regarding their preferences and pain points. Businesses that actively seek and analyze feedback from customers gain a deeper understanding of what drives purchasing decisions and how their products or services can be improved. This knowledge allows leaders to tailor their offerings to better meet market demands. This leads to improved customer satisfaction and loyalty. Leveraging customer insights can lead to more effective marketing strategies, ensuring that promotional efforts resonate with the target audience and ultimately drive sales.

Customer insights can also inspire innovation within the organization. Engaged customers are often willing to share their opinions and suggestions, which can inspire new ideas and help identify gaps in the market. By involving customers in the development process through surveys, focus groups, or co-creation initiatives, business leaders can create products and services that truly meet the needs of their audience. This proactive approach positions the company as responsive and customer-centric, enhancing its reputation and competitive edge.

Customer insights empower business leaders to make informed decisions that drive growth and ensure long-term success in a dynamic marketplace.

Collaborative Partnerships

Collaborative partnerships enable organizations to leverage complimentary strengths and resources, driving mutual growth and success. By forming alliances with suppliers, industry peers, non-profits, or community organizations, businesses can access new markets, technologies, and expertise that may not be available in-house. These partnerships foster innovation, as diverse teams can combine their knowledge and perspectives to develop creative solutions to complex challenges. Collaborative efforts can also enhance operational efficiencies, streamline processes, and reduce costs, ultimately contributing to a stronger competitive position in the marketplace.

Collaborative partnerships can enhance a company's reputation and credibility, particularly when engaging with stakeholders who share similar values and goals. By working together on projects that benefit the community or promote sustainability, businesses can show their commitment to corporate social responsibility, an approach which resonates well with consumers and investors alike. These partnerships also create opportunities for shared marketing and increased visibility, amplifying the reach and impact of all organizations involved.

Community Engagement and Innovation

Engaging with local communities can result in fresh ideas and perspectives. By actively taking part in community initiatives, businesses can show their commitment to social responsibility and contribute positively to the areas in which they operate. This engagement not only enhances the company's reputation but also builds trust and goodwill among community members, who often become loyal customers and brand advocates. Understanding the unique needs and values of the community can provide valuable insights that inform business practices and product offerings, ensuring that the company remains relevant and responsive to local demand.

This two-way interaction not only leads to innovative products that resonate with consumers but also empowers community members by giving them a voice in the development process. In a competitive landscape, companies that prioritize community engagement and innovation can differentiate themselves, create sustainable value, and foster long-term relationships that contribute to both business success and community well-being.

Risk Management and Compliance

In an increasingly regulated environment, maintaining healthy relationships with regulatory bodies is critical for risk management. Engaging with stakeholders like regulatory bodies, investors, and community groups, helps businesses identify, assess, and address risks that could affect their operations, reputation, and financial stability. By fostering open communication and transparency, leaders can build trust with stakeholders, reassuring them that the company prioritizes ethical practices and is committed to upholding standards. This proactive approach not only minimizes the likelihood of encountering legal issues or penalties, but also enhances the organization's credibility and resilience in the face of uncertainty.

Effective risk management and compliance strategies contribute to a company's long-term sustainability and competitive advantage. When business leaders actively engage with external stakeholders to understand their concerns and expectations, they can implement policies and practices that align with industry standards and societal values. This alignment not only protects the organization from potential risks but also positions it favorably in the eyes of customers and investors, who increasingly prioritize ethical and responsible business practices. By integrating risk management and compliance into their stakeholder engagement strategies, business leaders can create a culture of accountability and integrity that fosters loyalty and support, ultimately driving sustainable growth and success in a complex business environment.

Proactive Engagement

Proactively engaging with regulatory bodies can lead to a better understanding of compliance requirements and industry standards. Companies that maintain open lines of communication with regulators are more likely to receive guidance and support during audits or inspections. This proactive approach can help organizations stay ahead of regulatory changes and mitigate risks associated with non-compliance.

By actively reaching out to stakeholders—such as customers, suppliers, investors, and community members—business leaders can gather valuable insights and feedback that inform decision-making and enhance overall business strategies. This forward-thinking approach not only builds trust and strengthens relationships but also positions the company as a responsive and responsible entity that values stakeholder input. In an era where information moves faster than the speed of light, being proactive can help mitigate risks associated with negative perceptions or crises, ensuring that the business maintains a positive reputation.

Proactive engagement fosters innovation and collaboration by creating an open dialogue with stakeholders. When business leaders actively involve external parties in discussions about new products, services, or initiatives, they can tap into diverse perspectives and expertise that lead to creative solutions and improvements. This collaborative environment encourages stakeholder investment in the company's success, as they feel heard and valued in the decision-making process.

Crisis Management

In times of crisis, strong relationships with external stakeholders can be invaluable. Companies that have cultivated trust within their communities and regulatory bodies can more effectively manage crises. When a crisis occurs—be it a product recall, data breach, or public relations issue—how a company communicates and engages with its stakeholders can significantly affect its reputation and long-term viability.

By having a well-defined crisis management plan in place, business leaders can ensure timely and effective communication with customers, investors, suppliers, and the community. This proactive approach not only helps mitigate the immediate impact of the crisis but also demonstrates to stakeholders that the organization is committed to accountability and problem-solving, which is essential for maintaining their confidence and support.

Effective crisis management allows businesses to learn from challenges and strengthen their stakeholder relationships over time. Engaging stakeholders during a crisis provides valuable opportunities for feedback and dialogue, which can inform future strategies and risk management practices.

By involving stakeholders in the recovery process and addressing their concerns, business leaders can rebuild trust and loyalty, often emerging from a crisis with an even stronger reputation. In today's interconnected world, where information travels quickly, a strong crisis management strategy not only protects the organization during difficult times but also positions it for resilience and growth in the face of adversity. Ultimately, prioritizing crisis management ensures that businesses are better equipped to handle uncertainties while fostering long-term relationships built on trust and transparency.

Fostering Long-Term Sustainability

Sustainable business practices are becoming increasingly important to stakeholders across the board as they align corporate goals with the broader interests of society and the environment. By prioritizing sustainable practices, businesses can demonstrate their commitment to responsible stewardship of resources, which resonates positively with stakeholders, including customers, investors, and community members. In an era where consumers increasingly favor companies that prioritize environmental and social responsibility, engaging stakeholders in sustainability initiatives can enhance brand loyalty and attract new customers. Investors are increasingly assessing companies based on their sustainability performance, making it crucial for business leaders to integrate sustainable practices into their overall strategy to secure long-term investment and support.

Engaging stakeholders in sustainability efforts fosters collaboration and innovation, allowing businesses to leverage diverse perspectives and expertise. By working together with suppliers, local communities, and other partners, companies can identify new opportunities for sustainable practices that not only reduce environmental impact but also drive operational efficiencies and cost savings.

This collaborative approach can lead to the development of innovative products and services that meet evolving consumer demands while addressing pressing societal challenges. By fostering long-term sustainability through proactive stakeholder engagement, business leaders can create lasting value for their organizations while contributing to a healthier planet and stronger communities, ensuring their relevance and success in the future.

Environmental and Social Responsibility

Investors are increasingly seeking companies that demonstrate a commitment to environmental and social responsibility, as it shows a commitment to ethical practices that resonate with increasingly conscious consumers. In today's marketplace, stakeholders are more aware of the impact companies have on the environment and society. By actively engaging in environmentally sustainable practices and socially responsible initiatives, businesses can enhance their reputation, foster trust, and build loyalty among customers who prioritize these values. This not only differentiates a brand in a competitive landscape but also attracts investors looking for companies that align with their own ethical standards, ultimately driving financial performance and long-term sustainability.

By involving employees, customers, suppliers, and community members in sustainability efforts, companies can identify new opportunities for improving practices that benefit both the organization and the broader community. This collaborative approach can lead to innovative products and services that address environmental challenges while meeting consumer needs. Ultimately, by prioritizing environmental and social responsibility in their stakeholder engagement strategies, business leaders can create a positive impact that supports both organizational success and societal well-being, thereby ensuring their legacy and continued relevance in an evolving business landscape.

Community Impact

Businesses that invest in their local communities create a positive impact that extends beyond their operations. Through active engagement with the community and contributions to its development through initiatives such as local sponsorships, volunteer programs, and educational outreach, businesses can demonstrate their commitment to social responsibility. While this enhances the company's image, it also fosters goodwill among community members, who are more likely to support a business that actively invests in their welfare.

Additionally, focusing on community impact can yield valuable insights that inform business practices and product offerings. Engaging with community members allows business leaders to better understand local needs, preferences, and challenges, which can guide decision-making and innovation. This collaboration can lead to the development of products and services that resonate with the community, ensuring relevance and demand.

A strong community presence can attract talent, as employees are often drawn to organizations that prioritize social impact. Ultimately, by prioritizing community engagement and showing a genuine commitment to making a positive difference, business leaders can build sustainable relationships that not only enhance their brand reputation but also contribute to long-term success and resilience.

In summary, the value of business relationships with external stakeholders is multifaceted and profound. By enhancing reputation, driving innovation, managing risks, and fostering long-term sustainability, organizations can position themselves for success in an increasingly competitive landscape. The insights gained from engaging with customers, suppliers, investors, community members, and regulatory bodies are invaluable.

As the business environment continues to evolve, organizations that prioritize these relationships will not only thrive but also contribute positively to society as a whole. Leadership in the modern era is not just about directing internal operations; it's about forging connections that enrich the entire ecosystem in which a business operates. By understanding and valuing these external relationships, companies can ensure their relevance and success for years to come.

As we reflect on the strategic importance of external relationships, it becomes equally vital to examine the emotional and human dimensions of leadership. In times of uncertainty and rapid change, hope and compassion emerge as powerful forces that can unify teams, inspire action, and sustain resilience. The next chapter explores how these often-overlooked qualities are not only essential for creating a healthy organizational culture but also serve as guiding principles for leaders committed to long-term impact and meaningful progress.

Chapter 15

Inspiring Hope: The Role of Hope in Compassionate Leadership

"Compassionate leadership is about being able to connect with others and understand their needs."

– Maya Angelou

Leadership qualities such as intelligence, decisiveness, and strategic thinking have often dominated discussions about what makes an effective leader. However, the ability to inspire hope in others has risen to the forefront as the world becomes increasingly complicated and uncertain. Hope is not merely a fleeting emotion; it is a powerful motivator that can inspire teams, foster resilience, and create a culture of compassion and collaboration.

Compassionate leadership goes beyond simply understanding the needs of others; it encompasses a deep emotional connection that inspires trust and loyalty. Hope acts as a catalyst in this relationship, encouraging leaders to envision a brighter future for their teams and to instill a sense of purpose even in challenging times. By fostering an environment where hope thrives, leaders empower their teams to overcome obstacles, adapt to change, and pursue shared goals with renewed determination.

As leaders embody hope, they create a ripple effect that influences the attitudes and behaviors of their followers. This chapter will explore how hopeful leaders foster resilience, enabling their teams to navigate uncertainty with a constructive mindset. The act of instilling hope involves more than mere optimism; it requires empathy and an authentic commitment to the well-being of others. Compassionate leaders who articulate a hopeful vision not only enhance individual morale but also cultivate a collective spirit that drives collaboration and innovation.

The interplay between hope and compassion can transform organizational culture. This chapter explores how leaders can intentionally cultivate hope within their teams, creating an atmosphere where individuals feel valued and inspired. Through case studies and practical strategies, we will highlight the importance of hope as a foundational element in compassionate leadership, illustrating its profound impact on team dynamics, performance, and overall organizational success. Through this exploration, I aim to show that hope is not just a passive emotion but an active force that leaders can harness to elevate their influence and create meaningful change.

Understanding Compassionate Leadership

Before exploring the importance of hope, it is essential to define what compassionate leadership entails. Compassionate leaders prioritize empathy, care, and understanding in their interactions with team members. They focus on the well-being of their employees while also driving organizational goals. This dual focus creates an environment where individuals feel valued, supported, and motivated to contribute their best work.

Compassionate leadership is characterized by several key traits:

1. Empathy

The ability to understand and share the feelings and perspectives of others, allowing individuals to connect on an emotional level. It involves recognizing and validating another person's experiences, emotions, and thoughts, which fosters compassion and enhances interpersonal relationships. Empathy goes beyond mere sympathy, it requires active engagement and a deep comprehension of another's situation, enabling one to respond appropriately and supportively. Ultimately, empathy plays a crucial role in promoting kindness, cooperation, and social harmony.

2. Active Listening

A communication technique that involves fully concentrating, understanding, responding to, and remembering what the speaker is saying. It requires the listener to engage with the speaker by providing feedback, asking clarifying questions, and reflecting on the content to ensure comprehension. This practice goes beyond simply hearing words; it emphasizes empathy and presence, allowing the listener to create a supportive environment where the speaker feels valued and understood. By fostering open dialogue and reducing misunderstandings, active listening enhances interpersonal relationships and promotes effective communication.

3. Supportiveness

The quality of being encouraging, helpful, and understanding toward others, fostering an environment where individuals feel valued and understood. It involves actively offering emotional, mental, or practical assistance to someone in need, whether through words of encouragement, empathetic listening, or tangible help. Supportiveness is characterized by a non-judgmental attitude, patience, and a willingness to be present for others during challenging times. This nurturing behavior enhances trust and strengthens relationships, promoting resilience and well-being among individuals and groups.

4. Integrity

The quality of being honest and having strong moral principles that guide an individual's actions and decisions. It encompasses consistency between one's values, beliefs, and behaviors, ensuring that a person acts ethically and transparently in all situations. Integrity involves taking responsibility for one's actions, maintaining accountability, and adhering to a code of conduct, even when faced with challenges or temptations. This commitment to moral uprightness builds trust and respect in relationships, both personal and professional. It also plays a key role in creating and maintaining a positive and principled environment.

The Power of Hope

Hope is a foundational trait that enhances these characteristics, making compassionate leaders more effective. When leaders embody hope, they create a positive vision for the future that inspires both themselves and their teams. This optimistic outlook encourages leaders to understand and appreciate the emotions and perspectives of others, fostering deeper empathy. Leaders who exude hope are more likely to emotionally connect with their team members, as they can envision possibilities for growth and improvement, which in turn helps them relate to the challenges and aspirations of those they lead.

Hope motivates leaders to engage fully with their team members. When leaders believe in the potential for positive change, they are more inclined to pay attention to the ideas and concerns expressed by others. This attentiveness not only validates the speaker's feelings but also opens the door for meaningful dialogue and collaboration. Active listening, underpinned by hope, allows leaders to truly understand the needs and motivations of their teams, fostering an environment where everyone feels heard and valued. This creates a culture of open communication that bolsters team cohesion and drives collective progress.

In addition, hope enhances supportiveness and integrity within compassionate leadership. Leaders who are hopeful are more likely to provide emotional and practical support to their team members, believing in their capabilities and potential to overcome challenges. This supportive attitude cultivates trust and loyalty, as employees feel encouraged to share their struggles and aspirations.

Hope reinforces integrity, as leaders who maintain a hopeful perspective are more committed to ethical behavior and decision-making. They are driven by a vision of what could be, which aligns their actions with their values, ensuring consistency and authenticity in their leadership.

Ultimately, hope is a catalyst for fostering a compassionate leadership style that nurtures empathy, active listening, supportiveness, and integrity, creating a harmonious and effective organizational culture.

The Nature of Hope

Hope, in its simplest form, is the belief that a better future is possible, even when the present feels uncertain or overwhelming. It is more than mere wishful thinking; hope is an active, intentional mindset that involves setting meaningful goals, cultivating the motivation to pursue them, and maintaining a sense of agency over the outcomes.

From a psychological standpoint, hope has been linked to numerous positive outcomes, including improved mental health, enhanced resilience, and greater overall well-being. In the realm of leadership, these benefits take on even deeper significance. Leaders who embody hope serve as beacons for their teams, guiding others through turbulence with a steady vision of what lies ahead.

A hopeful leader does not ignore challenges; rather, they face them head-on while maintaining the belief that progress is possible. This perspective becomes the lens through which they evaluate problems, make decisions, and communicate with others. It is not just about maintaining a positive attitude; it is about inspiring others to believe in a future they can help shape. When a leader radiates hope, that energy spreads. It is contagious. It lifts the collective spirit of a team, reenergizes stalled momentum, and offers people something to rally around.

Inspiring Motivation and Resilience

Perhaps one of the most transformative effects of hope is its power to motivate. When leaders communicate a hopeful outlook, they give their teams a reason to believe that their efforts matter—that what they are working toward is achievable and worthwhile. During difficult times, when morale dips and uncertainty rises, hope becomes a stabilizing force. Imagine a leader navigating a severe downturn, whether due to market conditions, a global crisis, or an internal shake-up. A compassionate leader, rather than retreating or sugarcoating, addresses the truth while painting a picture of recovery, growth, and purpose. This reframing can shift an entire team's mindset from despair to determination.

Hope also fortifies resilience. In workplaces, setbacks are inevitable. Projects fail, plans derail, and change disrupts familiar rhythms. Leaders who foster hope give their teams the mental and emotional tools to bounce back. Studies show that hopeful individuals are more adept at problem-solving and more likely to persist through obstacles. This resilience is not just about endurance; it is about learning, adapting, and pressing forward with confidence. Within organizations, resilience built on a foundation of hope leads to teams that do not just survive hard seasons—they evolve through them.

Enhancing Emotional Well-Being

Beyond performance and outcomes, hope has a profound impact on emotional well-being. In a workplace where leaders express hope openly and consistently, team members often feel more secure, supported, and optimistic about their future. Emotional well-being becomes a shared experience, rather than an individual responsibility. People are more engaged, more connected to their work, and more willing to invest themselves fully in the mission at hand.

A hopeful workplace culture is one where people feel psychologically safe, safe to express themselves, safe to fail, and safe to grow. When a leader listens with empathy, encourages open dialogue, and models a hopeful perspective, they create a ripple effect. That emotional tone spreads, infusing the workplace with a sense of belonging. People begin to believe not just in the work, but in each other. They know they are not alone in facing challenges, and that sense of connection bolsters morale and enhances productivity.

Cultivating a Positive Organizational Culture

Hope is not just an emotion, it is an engine that drives culture. When leaders integrate hope in their leadership philosophy, they shape environments where creativity and innovation thrive. Teams feel empowered to take risks, try new ideas, and speak openly without fear of judgment or failure. This openness fuels collaboration and forward momentum.

In contrast, environments devoid of hope often become rigid, risk-averse, and disconnected. Fear replaces trust, productivity dips, innovation stalls, and turnover increases. Hopeful leaders counter this by consistently reinforcing a shared sense of purpose and progress. They cultivate a sense of belonging, highlight small wins, and remind their teams that every step forward matters. Over time, this intentional nurturing of hope transforms the organizational culture into one that is not only productive but also deeply human.

Promoting Empathy and Understanding

Hope and empathy go hand in hand. A hopeful leader recognizes that people are not machines, they have stories, struggles, and aspirations. This understanding fosters an environment where listening becomes a leadership skill, not just a soft skill. When a leader pauses to understand the unique perspectives of each team member, they send a clear message: you matter, and your experience matters.

Empathy deepens trust. In moments of difficulty, be it personal hardship or professional setbacks—leaders who respond with empathy and hope can help team members navigate their challenges without feeling isolated or diminished. They create a culture where people are encouraged to ask for help, where vulnerability is met with support rather than judgment. In doing so, they build a resilient, united workforce that stands stronger together.

Encouraging Growth and Learning

Hopeful leaders also frame challenges not as dead ends, but as stepping stones. They encourage their teams to approach setbacks with curiosity rather than fear. This mindset is central to growth. When employees feel safe to experiment, fail, and try again, learning becomes part of the daily rhythm. Leaders who model this attitude open the door for innovation.

Consider a leader launching a new initiative that does not immediately meet expectations. Rather than scrapping it or placing blame, a hopeful leader invites reflection: What worked? What did not? What can we try next? This approach transforms failure from something to be avoided into something to be learned from. The result is an agile, empowered workforce that thrives on improvement and continuous learning.

Facilitating Change and Adaptability

Finally, hope is essential in leading through change. Today's business environment is anything but static. New technologies, shifting markets, and evolving customer needs gives organizations no choice but to pivot quickly. Change often stirs up fear and resistance, but hope helps teams move forward with clarity and confidence despite the severity of the change.

Hopeful leaders paint a compelling picture of what lies beyond the disruption. They do not ignore uncertainty, but they emphasize possibility and opportunity. They guide their teams through transitions with honesty, support, and an unwavering belief in what can be achieved together. In doing so, they transform change from a threat into an opportunity. Adaptability becomes not just a response to pressure, but a proactive pursuit of growth.

Hope is not merely an abstract concept; it is a vital trait that shapes the effectiveness of compassionate leaders. By inspiring motivation and resilience, enhancing growth, and facilitating change, hope serves as a cornerstone of successful leadership. In a world fraught with uncertainty and complexity, compassionate leaders who embody hope can create environments where individuals feel valued, supported, and motivated to contribute their best work.

As organizations continue to navigate the challenges of the modern world, the role of hope in leadership will only become more significant. Leaders who prioritize hope as a core trait will not only enhance their effectiveness but also foster a culture of compassion and resilience within their teams. Ultimately, the power of hope can transform organizations, making them more adaptable, innovative, and successful in achieving their goals.

The power of hope and compassion in leadership is not merely theoretical—it is vividly embodied in the lives of those who have led through some of history's most intense and high-stakes situations. Few leaders exemplify this more profoundly than Lieutenant General Hal Moore. In the crucible of combat, where fear and uncertainty reign, Moore demonstrated unwavering hope, deep compassion for his soldiers, and an unshakable commitment to their well-being. His ability to lead under fire offers timeless lessons in courage, clarity, and character, principles that remain relevant far beyond the battlefield. In the next chapter, we will explore how Moore's example reveals the true heart of leadership: one that inspires trust, builds unity, and leads with both strength and humanity.

Chapter 16

No One Left Behind: Leadership Lessons from Lieutenant General Hal Moore

"When we step onto the battlefield. I will be the first boots on and the last boots off."

–Lieutenant General Hal Moore

Lieutenant General Hal Moore is a name synonymous with exemplary military leadership. Known for his bravery, strategic acumen, and profound insight into the human aspects of leadership. His experiences, particularly during the Vietnam War, provide a treasure trove of lessons applicable not only in military contexts but also in various leadership environments, including business, education, and community service. In this chapter, we will explore the key leadership lessons drawn from General Moore's life and career, illustrating how his principles can inspire and guide both current and future leaders.

The Battle of Ia Drang

Fought from November 14 to 18, 1965, the Battle of Ia Drang was one of the first major engagements between American forces and the North Vietnamese Army (NVA) during the Vietnam War. It took place in the Ia Drang Valley in the Central Highlands of Vietnam and involved the 1st Battalion, 7th Cavalry Regiment, supported by air cavalry units. The battle began with a helicopter assault, marking the first large-scale use of air mobility in combat. The American forces, led by Lieutenant Colonel Hal Moore, aimed to establish a foothold in the area and disrupt NVA operations.

As the battle unfolded, the United States troops found themselves engaged in intense fighting against a well-coordinated NVA force. The NVA employed effective tactics, including ambushes and concentrated fire, leading to significant casualties on both sides. Despite being outnumbered, the American forces demonstrated resilience and adaptability, utilizing air support and maintaining communication to coordinate their defense. The battle featured fierce close-quarters combat, with soldiers on both sides displaying extraordinary bravery under fire.

The Battle of Ia Drang concluded with a tactical victory for the United States, as its forces managed to inflict heavy casualties on the NVA and hold their positions. However, it also highlighted the challenges of fighting in Vietnam, including the difficulties of navigating the terrain and the complexities of guerrilla warfare. This battle had lasting implications, shaping United States military strategy and public perception of the Vietnam War. The experiences and lessons learned at Ia Drang would influence future engagements and contribute to the evolving nature of the conflict.

Lieutenant General Hal Moore

Hal Moore was a notable American military officer, best known for his leadership during the Vietnam War. Born on February 13, 1922, in Bardstown, Kentucky, he graduated from the United States Military Academy at West Point in 1945. Moore's early career included various assignments in the United States Army, but his most significant contributions came during the Vietnam War, particularly as the commander of the 1st Battalion, 7th Cavalry Regiment during the Battle of Ia Drang in November 1965, a pivotal moment in the war.

The Battle of Ia Drang showcased Moore's exceptional leadership skills and innovative tactics. Despite being heavily outnumbered, he successfully coordinated air and ground forces, demonstrating the effectiveness of air mobility in combat. His bravery and strategic acumen resulted in a hard-fought victory, although it came at a high cost, with significant casualties on both sides. The battle's outcomes were extensively studied and have had a lasting impact on military tactics and strategy. Moore's actions during this engagement earned him widespread recognition and respect, and he became a symbol of American military leadership during the Vietnam War.

After the war, Hal Moore continued to serve in various capacities, eventually retiring as a lieutenant general. Moore's contributions to military strategy and his commitment to his soldiers have been honored through numerous awards and accolades, leaving a lasting impact on both military history and the lives he influenced throughout his career. He passed away on February 10, 2021, but remains a revered figure in American military history.

The Importance of Preparation

One of the most profound lessons from General Hal Moore's leadership is the centrality of preparation, not as a reactive measure, but as a foundational principle. During the Battle of Ia Drang in 1965, Moore did not rely solely on instinct or improvisation. Instead, he brought his men into battle with months of training, carefully rehearsed strategies, and a clear understanding of possible contingencies. This level of forethought and discipline proved to be a decisive factor when his unit faced overwhelming enemy forces and rapidly shifting battlefield conditions.

Preparation is the bedrock of effective leadership in any context, military or civilian. Leaders who fail to prepare not only set themselves up for failure but also compromise the success and safety of their teams. Strategic foresight allows leaders to anticipate obstacles, reduce uncertainty, and make informed decisions when the unexpected arises. It creates the foundation upon which resilience and agility are built.

In modern organizational settings, preparation translates into creating comprehensive project plans, conducting risk assessments, scenario planning, and equipping team members with the necessary tools and training. Leaders who invest time in preparation cultivate a culture of readiness. Their teams are more confident, capable, and collaborative, able to face challenges with clarity and purpose rather than panic or confusion.

Leading by Example

General Moore's legacy is deeply rooted in his conviction to lead from the front. He did not command from a distance; he stood shoulder-to-shoulder with his soldiers, sharing in their hardships, risks, and sacrifices. His presence on the battlefield was more than symbolic—it demonstrated his commitment to the values he preached. This courage and consistency earned him the deep respect and loyalty of his troops, reinforcing the belief that he would never ask anything of them that he would not do himself.

The concept of leading by example extends far beyond the battlefield. In business and organizational leadership, it means embodying the standards you expect from others. A leader who demands accountability but avoids responsibility, or who preaches transparency but withholds information, creates dissonance and distrust. By contrast, when leaders model integrity, work ethic, and humility, they set the tone for the entire team.

Employees closely watch their leaders' behavior. When they see alignment between words and actions, trust deepens and team cohesion strengthens. Leaders who lead by example inspire others to rise to the same standard. This alignment builds credibility and sets the foundation for a values-driven culture that encourages excellence, respect, and collective ownership of results.

The Value of Communication

Throughout the chaos of the Ia Drang Valley, Moore understood that effective communication could mean the difference between survival and disaster. He maintained constant communication with his units, shared critical updates in real time, and ensured that every soldier knew their role in the mission. His communication was clear, direct, and consistent, even under fire, which kept his team aligned and grounded amid the fog of war.

In any organization, communication is the glue that holds teams together. A lack of transparency or poor messaging can lead to confusion, mistrust, and disengagement. Leaders must take the time to not only share information but also to listen. Open lines of communication help teams remain aligned, encourage problem-solving, and foster a sense of shared purpose. This is especially important during times of change, crisis, or uncertainty.

Good communication also builds relational capital. When leaders are approachable and honest, employees are more likely to bring up concerns early, offer new ideas, and collaborate cross-functionally. Tools such as regular team check-ins, feedback loops, and transparent decision-making processes allow communication to become not just a function of leadership—but a defining characteristic of an inclusive and agile culture.

Building Trust and Loyalty

General Moore's leadership was defined by the deep trust and loyalty he built with his soldiers. He did not demand loyalty, it was earned through consistent care, fairness, and presence. He made it clear that his primary responsibility was the safety and success of his troops, and they, in turn, committed to giving their best for him and for each other. This mutual trust became a critical asset when the stakes were highest.

In civilian leadership, trust remains a powerful currency. Teams that trust their leader communicate more openly, support one another, and stay committed even through adversity. Loyalty is not created through motivational speeches alone, it is developed over time through authentic relationships, transparency, and a leader's willingness to advocate for their team.

Leaders build trust through daily actions, by following through on commitments, showing empathy in challenging times, and recognizing the contributions of others. When employees feel seen, valued, and supported, they invest themselves fully in their work. This creates a positive feedback loop where trust breeds loyalty, and loyalty in turn fosters stronger performance and deeper engagement.

Decision-Making Under Pressure

Moore's ability to make swift, sound decisions under immense pressure was instrumental during the Battle of Ia Drang. Faced with incomplete information, limited resources, and rapidly evolving threats, he demonstrated remarkable clarity and composure. His decisions were not haphazard—they were rooted in rigorous preparation, experience, and a calm assessment of the situation. This capacity to lead decisively under fire saved lives and helped secure strategic outcomes.

In the business world, the pressure may not be life-or-death, but the stakes can still be high, possibly in the form of product launches, crisis response, major investments, or public reputation. Leaders must develop the mental discipline to stay composed under stress and the analytical skill to process information quickly. This often means creating mental models and frameworks in advance, so when pressure hits, decision-making becomes more structured and less reactive.

Training for these moments involves simulation, mentorship, and learning from both failure and success. Decision-making under pressure improves when leaders practice evaluating trade-offs, gathering diverse input, and trusting their team's capabilities. Strong leaders do not freeze or panic, they lean into their preparation and respond with courage, guided by values and critical thinking.

Empowering Others

Moore recognized that effective leadership was not about commanding every action, it was about preparing and empowering others to lead themselves. On the battlefield, he trusted his officers and soldiers to act independently when needed, enabling them to respond quickly to threats without waiting for orders. This decentralization of decision-making allowed his unit to be agile and responsive, a key factor in their survival and success.

In the workplace, empowering others involves giving employees the autonomy, resources, and authority to take ownership of their work. Micromanagement stifles innovation and breeds dependency. Empowerment, on the other hand, fuels confidence and drives performance. When leaders trust their people to make decisions, they unlock new levels of engagement and creativity.

Empowerment also enables leadership development at every level. It encourages initiative, accountability, and continuous improvement. By cultivating a culture where team members are not only permitted but encouraged to lead within their roles, organizations become more resilient, adaptive, and ready to meet future challenges with a strong internal bench of capable leaders.

Adaptability and Flexibility

General Moore knew that no matter how carefully a plan is crafted, reality often demands change. In the unpredictable environment of combat, adaptability became essential. Moore's ability to pivot strategies in response to shifting conditions helped his forces maintain the upper hand. His mindset, rooted in preparation but open to change, allowed him to seize opportunities and mitigate threats in real time.

In business, change is a constant. Market trends shift, technologies evolve, and crises emerge. Leaders who resist change risk becoming obsolete. Flexibility is not about abandoning structure, it is about being responsive and iterative. Adaptable leaders embrace feedback, adjust course when data demands it, and model a mindset of learning rather than rigidity.

Creating a culture of adaptability starts with the leader. It involves encouraging experimentation, rewarding flexibility, and de-stigmatizing failure. When employees see leaders adjust their own behaviors and strategies, they feel safer doing the same. This agility allows organizations to weather disruption, capitalize on innovation, and remain competitive in an ever-changing landscape.

The Role of Humility

Despite his rank and accomplishments, General Moore remained humble. He never led from ego or personal ambition, but from a genuine desire to serve his troops and fulfill his mission. He credited his team for their successes and took personal responsibility for setbacks. This humility made him approachable and trustworthy, enhancing the loyalty and effectiveness of his unit.

Humility is often undervalued, yet it is among the most important traits of a good leader. Humble leaders listen more than they speak, seek feedback, and are willing to admit mistakes. They create space for others to shine, which strengthens team performance and morale. Humility allows leaders to continuously grow and improve, rather than becoming stagnant or defensive.

Humility also fosters inclusivity and collaboration. When a leader does not feel threatened by others' expertise or opinions, they can build more diverse, high-functioning teams. In today's complex organizations, the best solutions often come from collective intelligence, not top-down mandates. Humble leaders make space for that collective intelligence to flourish.

Learning from Failure

General Moore never viewed failure as the end, he saw it as a vital part of the leadership journey. When things went wrong, he did not shift blame. Instead, he took ownership, debriefed thoroughly, and used every misstep as a stepping stone to improvement. This mindset allowed him and his units to evolve quickly and avoid repeating mistakes in future missions.

In any organization, failure is inevitable. The difference lies in how leaders respond. Leaders who view failure with shame or defensiveness create fear-based cultures. But those who embrace it as a learning opportunity foster environments where creativity, experimentation, and growth are possible. Teams that are free to fail are free to innovate.

A culture that learns from failure requires intentional practices: after-action reviews, open forums for reflection, and psychological safety. Leaders must model these behaviors by sharing their own failures transparently and demonstrating what they have learned. When teams see failure treated as data rather than defeat, they become more resilient, more agile, and more committed to continuous improvement.

Lieutenant General Hal Moore's leadership legacy offers more than just battlefield strategy, it provides a blueprint for courageous, compassionate, and effective leadership in any arena. His unwavering commitment to preparation, his example-driven leadership, his emphasis on trust, clear communication, and adaptability, all reflect qualities that resonate deeply with the demands of modern leadership. Moore's approach was not about commanding from the top—it was about serving, empowering, and standing alongside his people. These principles are not relics of military history—they are vital tools for today's leaders navigating uncertainty, disruption, and the ever-shifting dynamics of the modern workplace.

In particular, Moore's lessons hold powerful relevance for those leading Millennial and Generation Z workforces. These generations value authenticity, inclusivity, and purpose, qualities that Moore exemplified in abundance. His emphasis on mentorship, trust-building, and collaborative decision-making aligns with what younger employees seek in leadership. They do not merely want to be managed—they want to be inspired, empowered, and involved. Moore's leadership style, rooted in humility and integrity, fosters the kind of culture where innovation flourishes and individuals feel seen, supported, and challenged to grow.

As we transition to the next chapter, we move from the disciplined preparation and relational strength of Hal Moore to the unshakable resolve of another towering leader: Winston Churchill. If Moore teaches us how to lead with readiness and empathy, Churchill reminds us of the importance of unwavering persistence. In a world full of setbacks, ambiguity, and high stakes, the ability to never give in, to press forward with courage and conviction, is often the defining trait of extraordinary leadership. We now explore how Churchill's enduring defiance in the face of adversity offers a timeless lesson in perseverance.

Chapter 17

"Never Give In!"
The Unyielding Spirit & Leadership
of Winston Churchill

*"Continuous effort – not strength or intelligence – is
the key to unlocking our potential."*

– Winston Churchill

Leadership is often defined by the ability to make tough decisions, inspire others, and navigate challenges resiliently. One historical figure who embodies these qualities is Sir Winston Churchill. As a leader during one of the most tumultuous times in modern history, Churchill's steadfastness and refusal to capitulate under pressure offer invaluable lessons for contemporary business leaders. This chapter explores the significance of not giving in, drawing parallels between Churchill's leadership during World War II and the changes faced by modern business leaders.

The Battle of Britain

Fought between July and October 1940, the Battle of Britain had a profound psychological impact on the residents of London. As the German Luftwaffe launched relentless bombing raids, known as the Blitz, the city became a scene of destruction and despair. The constant threat of air raids instilled fear and anxiety among the population, forcing many to seek refuge in underground shelters. This environment of uncertainty created a collective trauma, as families faced the daily reality of loss, both of loved ones and their homes.

Despite the dire circumstances, Londoners, under the leadership of Winston Churchill, displayed remarkable resilience. The communal spirit strengthened as neighbors came together to support one another through shared adversity. People adapted to their new reality, often finding moments of joy and solidarity amid the chaos. The iconic phrase "Keep Calm and Carry On" emerged as a mantra, embodying the determination of residents to persevere despite the constant bombings. This resilience united the beleaguered population, and filled them with purpose.

The Historical Context of Churchill's Leadership

To appreciate the essence of Churchill's unyielding spirit, we must first understand the context in which he operated. Churchill's leadership emerged during one of the most tumultuous periods in modern history, characterized by the rise of totalitarian regimes and the impending threat of global conflict. Born in 1874 into a prominent aristocratic family, Churchill's early career spanned various roles, including soldier, journalist, and politician. His experiences in both World War I and the interwar period shaped his understanding of military strategy and diplomacy. By the time he became Prime Minister in 1940, Europe was on the brink of devastation, with Nazi Germany expanding its influence and threatening the very fabric of democracy.

Churchill's leadership style was marked by his oratory prowess and indomitable spirit, qualities that resonated deeply with the British public during World War II. His famous speeches rallied a nation grappling with fear and uncertainty. Churchill understood the importance of morale in warfare, using his communication skills to inspire resilience and unity among the populace. His defiance of Hitler and commitment to the Allied cause not only galvanized Britain but also positioned him as a key figure on the world stage, ultimately leading to the formation of pivotal alliances with the United States and the Soviet Union.

The postwar period presented new challenges for Churchill, as he faced the task of rebuilding a war-torn nation and addressing the emerging Cold War dynamics. His vision for a united Europe and warnings about the Iron Curtain highlighted his foresight regarding the evolving geopolitical landscape. Although he was voted out of office in 1945, Churchill's legacy as a leader who embodied courage and determination during a crisis has endured. His historical significance lies not only in his wartime leadership but also in his ability to adapt to the changing political climate, making him a pivotal figure in both British and global history.

The Importance of Resilience in Leadership

Resilience is a core quality of effective leaders, particularly in times of crisis. Churchill's leadership style was characterized by his unwavering commitment to his principles. He famously stated, "Success is not final, failure is not fatal: It is the courage to continue that counts." This philosophy highlights the importance of perseverance, a trait that business leaders must cultivate.

In the business world, leaders often face challenges that test their resolve. Economic downturns, competitive pressures, and internal conflicts can create an environment where giving in may seem like an easy option. However, like Churchill, effective leaders recognize that genuine success lies in standing firm and navigating through adversity.

The Power of Vision and Communication

Churchill was particularly adept at communicating a clear vision. He understood that in times of uncertainty, people look for direction. His speeches, filled with vivid imagery and stirring rhetoric, motivated the British public to remain steadfast. For instance, his declaration that he would "never surrender" became a rallying cry for the nation.

In the business realm, effective communication is equally vital. Leaders must articulate their vision and inspire their teams to remain committed to collective goals, even in the face of challenges. By fostering a culture of resilience and determination, leaders can encourage their teams to push through difficulties rather than succumb to despair.

Building a Culture of Determination

Churchill's leadership was not solely about his personal resolve; it was also about instilling a sense of determination in his followers. He surrounded himself with individuals who shared his commitment to victory. This collaborative spirit was crucial in fostering a culture of resilience.

Business leaders can take a page from Churchill's playbook by promoting a similar culture within their organizations. Encouraging open dialogue, recognizing effort, and celebrating small victories can motivate teams to stay focused and committed. When employees feel valued and part of a larger mission, they are less likely to give in when faced with obstacles.

Learning from Failure

One of Churchill's most remarkable traits was his ability to learn from failure. During his early political career, he faced numerous setbacks, including military defeats and political missteps. Instead of allowing these failures to deter him, Churchill used them as stepping stones to refine his strategies and strengthen his resolve.

In the business landscape, failure is often seen as a stigma. However, effective leaders understand that failure is an integral part of the journey. By embracing a growth mindset and viewing setbacks as opportunities for learning, leaders can cultivate resilience not only in themselves but also in their teams. This shift in perspective encourages innovation and risk-taking, essential components for success.

The Role of Integrity and Ethics

Churchill's unyielding spirit was deeply rooted in his sense of integrity and ethics. He believed in fighting for justice and freedom, and this belief guided his decisions throughout the war. This moral compass not only earned him respect, but also galvanized the nation to rally behind a shared cause.

In business, ethical leadership is paramount. Leaders who exhibit integrity inspire trust and loyalty among their employees, stakeholders, and customers. By standing firm in their values and refusing to compromise on ethical standards, leaders can create an environment where resilience flourishes. A company grounded in strong ethics is more likely to weather storms and emerge stronger.

The Legacy of Churchill's Leadership

The legacy of Winston Churchill is a powerful testament to what leadership looks like when courage triumphs over fear and conviction eclipses convenience. In an age where many are quick to retreat at the first sign of resistance, Churchill reminds us that greatness is forged in the crucible of adversity. His leadership was not merely about wartime strategy or stirring speeches—it was about embodying a spirit so unquenchable that it shone bright even during the darkest hour.

Today's leaders, though often facing different kinds of battles, are no less challenged. Economic instability, rapid technological shifts, social upheaval, and the pressure to innovate under scrutiny have created a climate where resilience is not just admirable, it is essential. In boardrooms, startups, nonprofits, and community organizations, the call to lead with steadfastness in the face of uncertainty echoes Churchill's enduring message: never give in. His example urges today's leaders to resist the temptation of quick fixes, to hold to a long-term vision even when the present is chaotic, and to make bold decisions grounded in principle rather than popularity.

Churchill's legacy also challenges leaders to foster cultures where perseverance is a shared value, where teams are encouraged to push through setbacks, recalibrate after failures, and maintain belief in a shared mission. It is in these environments that innovation thrives, trust deepens, and meaningful progress takes root. His life proves that leadership is not about avoiding difficulty, but about rising to meet it with clarity, courage, and character.

Churchill did not just lead a nation through war; he left behind a blueprint for enduring leadership, one built not on ease, but on endurance. In an era defined by disruption and distraction, his words still resonate: *"If you are going through hell, keep going."* That mantra, when embraced by modern leaders, becomes more than survival—it becomes the foundation of transformation.

Just as Churchill exemplified resilience and resolve in the face of overwhelming odds, another type of leadership, one rooted in imagination, vision, and bold creativity, can be seen in the legacy of Walt Disney. Where Churchill led through defiance and determination, Disney led through dreaming big and daring to create what had never been created before. His approach shows that effective leadership is not one-dimensional; it can also stem from the ability to envision a brighter future and inspire others to believe in it. In the next chapter, we explore how Disney's imaginative leadership transformed not just an industry, but the very way people experience joy, wonder, and storytelling.

Chapter 18

Leading with Vision and Perspective: The Disney Way

*"Around here, however, we do not look backwards for very long. We keep
moving forward, opening up new doors and doing new things, because
we are curious... and curiosity keeps leading us down new paths."*

– Walt Disney

As the summer of 1955 approached, the construction of Disneyland
was in its final, chaotic months. Walt Disney walked through the dusty,
unfinished streets of his soon-to-be dream park, taking in every detail
with an artist's eye. He was not merely inspecting a construction site,
he was stepping into the world he had been envisioning for years, one
where families would leave reality behind and immerse themselves in
something magical.

Beside him, his brother Roy trailed slightly behind, his mind preoccupied
with the numbers. The budget was stretched thin, and every day brought
new expenses. While Walt saw the park through the eyes of a storyteller,
Roy saw it through the eyes of an investor who needed to make sure this
ambitious project did not become a financial disaster.

As they reached Main Street, U.S.A., Walt slowed his pace, his gaze
rising toward the row of freshly installed shop windows. Something
was not right. The buildings had the quaint charm of a turn-of-the-
century small town, and the street was beginning to take shape, but the
placement of the windows bothered him, they were too high.

To any other observer, they might have looked perfectly normal, built to standard construction heights. But Walt was not thinking about standards, he was thinking about children. He imagined a little boy walking hand-in-hand with his parents, pressing his face against the glass of a toy shop, his eyes lighting up at the sight of spinning trains and stuffed animals. He imagined a little girl watching, mesmerized, as a soda jerk at the ice cream parlor scooped towering swirls of chocolate and vanilla.

But with the windows as they were, children would not be able to see inside. They would only see reflections of the sky and the tops of buildings. The magic would be hidden from them, locked behind glass built for adults to peer through. That was not the experience Walt had in mind.

Turning back toward the construction crew, he ordered the windows to be lowered. It was a seemingly minor change, just a matter of a few feet, but it was one of countless small adjustments that made Disneyland different from any place built before it. The windows had to invite children in, had to capture their imaginations, and had to be placed at a height where they could see the magic without having to be lifted up by their parents.

Roy, ever the businessman, took a deep breath. Adjusting every window meant extra work, extra time, and extra money. They were already racing against the clock to meet their July opening date, and changes like this only added to the stress. But Roy knew his brother well. Once Walt had a vision for something, there was no talking him out of it. This was not about money or deadlines, it was about storytelling, about making a place that truly felt special.

The adjustment was made. The shop windows of Main Street were lowered just enough so that young guests could see inside, and be drawn into the experience rather than feeling like spectators.

It was a small decision in the grand scheme of Disneyland's construction, yet it spoke to Walt's meticulous attention to detail. He understood something that few others in his position did: the magic is not just in the big things, it is in the small things that guests do not even realize were designed for them.

When Disneyland finally opened, Main Street, U.S.A., became the heart of the park, filled with the laughter and awe of visitors of all ages. Children pressed their noses against the glass of the candy shop, their eyes wide with excitement. They gazed into the windows of the Emporium, captivated by the animated displays inside. The change had worked.

Walt had once again proven that no detail was too small when it came to bringing dreams to life. And Roy, practical as ever, had once again ensured that those dreams had the support they needed to become reality.

The lowered windows of Main Street were not just a construction choice, they were a symbol of Disneyland itself: a place designed not just for adults, not just for children, but for the child inside everyone.

Great leadership is not just about managing people, processes, and profits. It is about creating a vision so compelling that it inspires others to believe, follow, and innovate. This type of leadership is heart-led, driven by empathy, creativity, and an unwavering commitment to making a meaningful impact. One of the most powerful examples of heart-led leadership comes from Walt Disney, whose visionary approach transformed the entertainment industry and redefined the concept of theme parks.

A seemingly small design decision at Disneyland, adjusting the height of storefront windows on Main Street, U.S.A., provides profound insights into effective leadership. This story, involving Walt Disney and his brother Roy Disney, highlights essential leadership principles that are as relevant in business today as they were in the creation of the most magical place on Earth. Through this example, we will explore the critical leadership values of vision, empathy, attention to detail, innovation, and inclusivity, which are at the heart of leading with purpose and passion.

I. Customer-Centric Vision: Seeing Through the Eyes of Others

Walt Disney always envisioned Disneyland as a place where people of all ages could step into a world of wonder, escaping the mundane and immersing themselves in magic. His ability to see things not only as they were but as they *could* be was a hallmark of his leadership.

During the development of Main Street, U.S.A., Walt and Roy walked through the area and observed the layout of the storefronts. Walt, ever the visionary, suddenly dropped to his knees to see what Main Street would look like from a child's perspective. What he saw changed everything— he realized that the shop windows were too high for children to see inside, excluding them from part of the experience. He immediately ordered changes to ensure that children, not just adults, could engage with the magic of the park.

This moment encapsulates a critical leadership principle: true vision requires seeing through the eyes of those you serve. Whether you are leading a team, running a company, or managing a project, considering the needs, challenges, and experiences of others, employees, customers, and stakeholders, ensures that your leadership is impactful and effective.

Leadership Lesson: Leading with a Customer-First Mindset

- Great leaders do not assume; they observe and experience.
- Empathy is essential for creating an inclusive and engaging environment.
- Design and decisions should be rooted in the perspective of the end-user.

II. Attention to Detail: The Little Things Matter

Walt Disney was known for his relentless attention to detail. He believed that magic lived in the small touches, the things most people would not consciously notice but would *feel* when experiencing his creations.

The decision to lower the windows on Main Street was not a grand structural change, it was a small adjustment. Yet, it had a significant impact on how children engaged with their surroundings. This illustrates that great leaders understand the importance of the details, from how they communicate to how they build experiences for customers and employees.

In business, details define excellence. Leaders who invest time in the small things, whether it is ensuring employees feel heard, refining a product for better user experience, or crafting a culture of inclusion, set themselves apart from the rest. The little things, when accumulated, shape the bigger picture.

Leadership Lesson: Mastering the Art of Detail-Oriented Leadership

- Success is built on the foundation of small, thoughtful actions.
- Attention to detail signals care, dedication, and a commitment to excellence.
- A leader's ability to notice and improve small aspects of the business can elevate the entire organization.

III. Empathy and Perspective-Taking: Walking in Others' Shoes

One of Walt's greatest strengths was his ability to put himself in the shoes of others. By kneeling to see the world from a child's viewpoint, he demonstrated an essential leadership skill: empathy.

Empathy in leadership means making decisions with an understanding of how they impact employees, customers, and stakeholders. It means listening, adapting, and leading with compassion. In today's workforce, leaders who practice empathy create environments where employees feel valued, respected, and motivated to contribute their best work.

Leadership Lesson: Cultivating an Empathetic Leadership Style

- Seeing the world through others' eyes leads to better decision-making.
- Empathy fosters a culture of inclusivity, trust, and collaboration.
- Understanding employees' perspectives can drive engagement and innovation.

IV. Balancing Vision with Practicality: The Role of Roy Disney

While Walt was the dreamer, Roy was the pragmatic businessman. Roy's role in Disney's success was equally important, as he ensured that Walt's ambitious ideas were financially viable and operationally sound.

When Walt decided to lower the windows on Main Street, Roy likely considered the cost and practicality of the change. However, he ultimately supported the decision because he understood that vision must be balanced with execution. Leaders must inspire with bold ideas, but they must also ground their decisions in reality to ensure sustainable success.

Leadership Lesson: Harmonizing Creativity and Practicality

- Every leader needs a balance between vision and execution.
- Strong operational strategies must support bold ideas.
- Collaboration between creative and analytical minds drives long-term success.

V. The Power of Continuous Innovation and Improvement

Disneyland's evolution never stopped at opening day. Walt famously said, *"Disneyland will never be completed. It will continue to grow as long as there is imagination left in the world."* Adjusting the windows was just one of many improvements made to enhance the guest experience.

Leaders who adopt a mindset of continuous innovation understand that improvement is an ongoing process. Companies that rest on past successes will eventually fall behind. The best leaders foster cultures that encourage creativity, experimentation, and iteration.

Leadership Lesson: Embracing a Growth-Oriented Mindset

- Organizations must evolve to stay relevant and impactful.
- Leaders should encourage a culture of curiosity and experimentation.
- The best ideas often come from incremental improvements, not just major overhauls.

VI. Creating Inclusive Environments: Making Magic for Everyone

By considering the experience of children, Walt ensured that Disneyland was a place for *everyone*. This philosophy extended throughout the park, from ride accessibility to storytelling that resonated with diverse audiences.

Modern leaders must also prioritize inclusivity, whether in workplace culture, product development, or customer engagement. Businesses that foster inclusive environments see higher employee satisfaction, better innovation, and stronger brand loyalty.

Leadership Lesson: The Strength of Inclusive Leadership

- Inclusive leaders design experiences, products, and workplaces for diverse audiences.
- Valuing different perspectives fosters innovation and stronger communities.
- A workplace where everyone feels seen and heard drives engagement and performance.

The Legacy of Heart-Led Leadership

Walt Disney's leadership legacy is a compelling illustration of what happens when vision is paired with empathy and relentless attention to detail. His capacity to lead with heart, not just head, reshaped the entertainment industry and built an organization that continues to delight and inspire generations. But Disney's legacy is not just about animation or amusement parks; he laid a blueprint for heart-led leadership that transcends industries and roles. Whether it is the story of lowering the windows on Main Street so children could see the displays, or obsessing over the placement of trash cans for convenience, Disney demonstrated that even the smallest decisions can leave a lasting impact when made with others in mind.

Yet heart-led leadership is not confined to visionaries like Disney. It exists in every leader who prioritizes people over ego, purpose over position, and service over self-interest. It is the school principal who learns every student's name, the hospital administrator who rounds the floors to understand frontline challenges, the manager who listens deeply before responding, and the CEO who values the lived experience of their team as much as the quarterly report. Leading with heart means being present, intentional, and invested in the human experience behind every objective. It means acknowledging that leadership is not just about driving outcomes, but about creating environments where people can thrive, belong, and contribute meaningfully.

As the world of work continues to evolve, so must our understanding of what it takes to lead effectively. In an age that demands innovation, inclusion, and authenticity, heart-led leadership is not a luxury, it is a necessity. The leaders who will shape the future are those who see through the eyes of others, act with compassion, and lead with courage. They do not just drive performance; they nurture purpose. And they do not just manage people; they elevate them.

So the next time you walk down Main Street, whether it is a literal one or a metaphorical path in your own leadership journey, pause and look at the world from the perspective of those you lead. Because that is where heart-led leadership begins: in the choice to care deeply, see clearly, and lead boldly.

As we turn the page to the next chapter, I invite you into my own leadership story, a journey shaped not merely by titles or milestones, but by failures, lessons, and defining moments of growth. It is a story of leading through uncertainty, learning to serve others before myself, and discovering that leadership is less about having the answers and more about asking the right questions. Join me as we explore what it truly means to lead from the inside out.

Chapter 19

My Solari Journey

"A true leader has the confidence to stand alone, the courage to make tough decisions, and the compassion to listen to the needs of others."

– Douglas McArthur

In January 2014, I was just settling into a new role as the regional vice president of a Phoenix-based nonprofit overseeing Arizona and Texas behavioral health operations. I was in line to be the successor to the current CEO, who was planning to retire within the next two years. At the same time, Solari had recently parted with their longtime CEO.

A headhunting group approached me to ask whom I believed would be a suitable candidate for the Solari CEO position. I gave them a short list of qualified professionals that I recommended they investigate. A few weeks later, they returned and requested another list. Then a few weeks after that, they came back again, this time to ask if I would be interested in interviewing for the CEO position. I said that I would have to think about it and consult my wife.

I spent a week mulling over the prospects of this position. I decided to interview to at least clear the air about Solari's shortcomings and what I thought the Board needed to do for Solari to exist. I really did not intend to leave my current role, but I believed in Solari's role within the community and felt that it had good bones. It just needed some tweaks to put it in a position to succeed.

In February 2014, I sat down with the Board of Directors and the headhunter. I was familiar with all of the Board members through my time at the State and at the managed care organization overseeing crisis services.

I started my interview with: "This organization has a lot of potential, but without significant changes at all levels, it will not exist in six months." Bold, right?

I did not need this job and was not sure if I wanted the job if given the opportunity. I went on to say that the organization's reputation was not suitable within the community or among other similar organizations. The Board of Directors structure was flawed, with all members having some level of vested interest in Solari's strategic decisions and a lack of community and unconflicted (perceived or real) representation.

I laid out a few items that needed to change quickly:

- The organization needed to reengage with their funders with complete transparency and humility.
- The Board composition needed to change to have diverse community representation.
- The bylaws needed to be revised to reflect the change in Board composition.
- The leadership needed a complete revamp with regards to employee engagement and company culture.
- The organization needed to restore trust among the community at large.

Stepping out of the interview with the board, it was clear the CEO position would go to the interim leader. A call was made to share the news: "Congratulations! You will definitely get the CEO job, as there's no way the board would select me at this point."

For a while, nothing more was heard, and life continued as usual in my current role. Then, in April 2014, the board chair of Solari pulled me aside at a conference. Sitting down, she acknowledged, "You were right; everything you shared was correct." She explained that the board had carefully evaluated those insights and unanimously agreed on the necessary changes—along with the belief that I should lead the effort as CEO. The news came as a shock. Taking time to process, the decision was not made immediately.

After returning home from the conference, the conversation was shared with my wife, who responded with hostility. Her stance was clear: do not take the job. In her view, the organization was a "sinking ship," and stepping in at that moment would risk both my reputation and career. While her concerns were fully understood—and some reservations existed—the possibility of turning things around could not be ignored. Against her wishes, I chose to accept the role. The mission and the vital role Solari played in the community were worth fighting for.

The journey officially began on July 7, 2014. By September, new bylaws were in place. By November, the board had expanded, with more than 50 percent of its members coming from the community. By June 2015, staff turnover had dropped from 38 percent to below 7 percent.

Over ten years later, our revenue has grown from $15 million to more than $94 million per year. Our staff has grown to more than 800 employees, turnover remains within industry norms, funder relationships are outstanding, and we maintain positive support from both community members and stakeholders.

Solari has been nationally recognized as a Top Workplace, a Top Remote Workplace and a Top Nonprofit by *USA Today*.

Solari has also received national culture excellence awards in the following categories:

- Innovation
- Leadership
- Purpose & Values
- Work-Life Flexibility
- Employee Appreciation
- Employee Well-Being
- Compensation & Benefits
- Professional Development

Looking back, the decision to take on the challenge of leading Solari was not just a career move—it was a leap of faith. The organization was facing immense pressure, burdened with structural issues, morale challenges, and the looming question of whether it could survive at all. Many saw a sinking ship. I saw an opportunity to lead with heart, to listen, to serve, to rebuild something not just functional, but meaningful. It was never about personal accolades; it was about people. It was about honoring the mission to inspire hope and crafting a culture where that hope was not just a message we delivered externally, but something we lived daily within the organization.

The transformation did not come from positional authority, it came from connection, consistency, and compassion. We invested in people first. We created space for honest conversations, rebuilt trust where it had eroded, and focused relentlessly on creating an environment where our team could grow, contribute, and lead with purpose. It was not a solo journey. It was a collective act of courage from a team that chose to believe in something bigger than themselves. Slowly but surely, that belief became momentum. That momentum became change. And that change reshaped our identity, from a troubled organization into a nationally recognized leader in behavioral health.

Today, when I reflect on Solari's turnaround, it is not the awards or accolades that define our success—it is the culture we have built and the lives we have impacted. It is knowing that we did not compromise our values for the sake of survival, we thrived because we led with them. That is the essence of heart-led leadership: showing up with purpose, acting with empathy, and leading in a way that centers humanity at every turn. As we move into the final chapter of this book, we will explore how these lessons culminate into a vision for leadership that is not only sustainable, but deeply transformational, for organizations, for communities, and for ourselves. Because ultimately, heart-led leadership is not a tactic. It is a legacy.

Chapter 20

Conclusion

As we conclude this exploration of heart-led leadership, it becomes clear that this approach is not a fleeting ideal but a necessary evolution in how we lead in today's complex, connected, and ever-changing world. The challenges facing modern organizations, rapid technological disruption, shifting generational values, and an increasing demand for inclusivity and authenticity—require leaders who are as emotionally intelligent as they are technically capable. Heart-led leadership offers a response that is both human centered and high impact.

Throughout this book, we have explored the essential components of leading with heart: empathy, authenticity, humility, inclusion, and purpose. These are not abstract concepts; they are practical, powerful tools that shape culture, deepen engagement, and create workplaces where people do not just perform—they thrive. As we turn our attention to how these principles apply in real time, one thing becomes certain: the most enduring and transformative leaders are those who choose to lead from the inside out—with courage, compassion, and conviction.

The Changing Landscape of Work

The nature of work is undergoing a profound transformation. Millennials and Generation Z now comprise the majority of the global workforce, and their expectations are reshaping leadership paradigms. These generations prioritize meaning over money, collaboration over competition, and flexibility over rigidity. They want to be part of something larger than themselves, an organization with a clear purpose, and leadership that reflects integrity and care. Leaders who fail to understand these shifts risk alienating the very talent they need to succeed.

Heart-led leadership aligns perfectly with this new reality. It bridges the gap between traditional corporate structures and the human needs of a dynamic, values-driven workforce. In a time where burnout, disengagement, and turnover are rampant, leaders who connect on a deeper level will build more resilient, loyal, and motivated teams. Embracing heart-led leadership is not just good for culture, it is essential for sustainability and growth in the modern workplace.

Empathy as a Cornerstone

Empathy lies at the core of effective leadership. It is more than just understanding, it is about stepping into someone else's experience and responding with care and action. In heart-led organizations, empathy shapes everything from communication and decision-making to performance reviews and crisis response. It is what transforms a transactional workplace into a transformational one.

Leaders who lead with empathy create teams that are more cohesive, resilient, and innovative. When people feel understood and supported, they are more willing to take risks, contribute ideas, and support their peers. Empathy fosters loyalty and trust, two ingredients essential for long-term success. In a post-pandemic world where mental health, psychological safety, and human connection are more important than ever, empathetic leadership is not optional, it is a moral and business imperative.

Authenticity and Vulnerability

Authenticity is the antidote to disengagement. In a world filled with curated images and polished facades, people are craving realness—especially from their leaders. When leaders are willing to share their struggles, admit their mistakes, and lead with transparency, they build a culture of psychological safety. Vulnerability is not weakness; it is a powerful connector that says, "I am human, just like you."

Heart-led leaders understand that authenticity breeds authenticity. When leaders show up as their whole selves, they give others permission to do the same. This leads to stronger relationships, higher engagement, and a more inclusive environment. Vulnerable leadership breaks down barriers and builds bridges, reminding us that leadership is not about perfection—it is about presence and honesty.

Purpose-Driven Work

Purpose used to be a "nice-to-have"; now it is a nonnegotiable. Today's employees want to know that their work matters, and that their organization is making a positive impact on the world. Heart-led leadership centers purpose at the core of every decision and interaction, guiding teams with a sense of mission that transcends profit margins and job titles.

When purpose is clear and shared, it becomes a rallying point that aligns strategy, culture, and execution. Employees who feel connected to a greater mission are more engaged, resilient, and willing to go above and beyond. Heart-led leaders cultivate this connection by consistently reinforcing the "why" behind the work, tying everyday tasks to long-term impact, and inviting everyone to play a meaningful role in the journey.

Building Inclusive Cultures

Heart-led leadership demands inclusivity, not as a checkbox but as a deeply held value. Inclusive leaders recognize that diversity of thought, background, and experience leads to stronger outcomes and a richer workplace culture. They are intentional about creating spaces where every voice is heard, valued, and respected.

True inclusivity requires more than policies; it requires presence. It means leaders must actively seek out differing perspectives, challenge bias, and create opportunities for underrepresented voices to lead and shape the future. Heart-led leaders know that inclusion strengthens community, builds innovation, and ensures that everyone feels like they belong—not in spite of their differences, but because of them.

The Role of Mentorship and Development

Heart-led leaders do not just manage, they mentor. They take an active role in the growth and development of others, seeing potential where others see limitations. This investment in people reflects a deep belief that leadership is about multiplying impact, not hoarding power. Mentorship becomes a vehicle for legacy, influence, and trust.

Whether through formal programs or informal conversations, heart-led leaders coach with compassion and accountability. They celebrate wins, provide honest feedback, and help their teams navigate setbacks with resilience. This kind of support fosters confidence and accelerates professional development, preparing the next generation of leaders to continue the cycle of servant, heart-led leadership for years to come.

The Impact of Technology

Technology is reshaping how we connect, collaborate, and lead. While digital tools offer efficiency and scale, they can also create emotional distance and miscommunication. Heart-led leadership leverages technology not to replace human connection, but to enhance it. This means being intentional about how and when we use tools to build relationships and community.

From virtual team-building to empathetic check-ins via video call, leaders can infuse humanity into digital spaces. Tools such as Slack, Zoom, and project management software can support, but not replace, the need for meaningful dialogue and recognition. The most effective leaders will find ways to bring warmth, clarity, and care into even the most tech-driven interactions, proving that empathy and efficiency are not mutually exclusive.

Measuring the Effectiveness of Heart-Led Leadership

In order to sustain heart-led leadership, organizations must learn how to measure its impact. Traditional KPIs like revenue and output are important, but they do not tell the full story. Metrics such as employee engagement, retention rates, psychological safety, and culture surveys offer a more complete picture of organizational health and leadership effectiveness.

Heart-led leadership is not about intangible ideals; it is about tangible outcomes rooted in human experience. Leaders should use tools such as 360-degree feedback, pulse surveys, and one-on-one development conversations to assess how their leadership is being received and learn where they can grow. By integrating both qualitative and quantitative data, organizations can refine their strategies and build environments where heart-led leadership is not only practiced but proven.

A Call to Action

As we step into a future defined by rapid change, increasing complexity, and rising expectations for ethical leadership, the call to action could not be clearer: heart-led leadership must become the new standard. This is not a feel-good philosophy reserved for the few, it is a strategic imperative for every leader, in every industry, at every level. If we are to build resilient, future-ready organizations, we must lead with empathy, model authenticity, anchor our actions on purpose, celebrate diversity, and relentlessly invest in the growth of others.

This shift requires more than policy changes or inspirational slogans. It calls for a courageous reimagining of what leadership looks and feels like. It challenges executives to model vulnerability, managers to mentor with compassion, and teams to hold one another accountable for creating inclusive, values-driven cultures. Most important, it requires each of us to ask the deeper question: *What kind of leader do I want to be remembered as?* The answer to that question will shape not just your leadership legacy, but the lives you influence along the way.

The Future of Heart-Led Leadership

The road ahead belongs to organizations that embrace this new paradigm, not just because it is ethical but because it works. Heart-led leadership will be a defining advantage in attracting, retaining, and energizing talent in an era where people are no longer content with transactional work environments. They seek purpose. They demand authenticity. They expect to be seen, not just as employees but as whole human beings.

The organizations that thrive tomorrow will be those that start building heart-led cultures today: cultures where courage is valued over control, where compassion fuels creativity, and where connection is seen not as a perk but as a path to performance. By embedding these principles into the DNA of our teams and systems, we can create organizations that are not only more effective but also more human and, ultimately, more enduring.

Leading What's Next

Leadership has always been about more than outcomes; it is about impact. It is about the lives we touch, the trust we build, and the legacy we leave. Heart-led leadership calls us to lead not with ego or fear, but with intention and humanity. It asks us to trade authority for influence, perfection for presence, and success for significance.

The choice is ours. We can continue managing through outdated models of control and hierarchy—or we can lead with heart and unlock a future filled with innovation, belonging, and lasting change. Let us be bold enough to lead differently. Let us be brave enough to care deeply. Let us build organizations where people thrive and where work becomes a place not just of productivity but of purpose.

This is the moment. This is the movement. It's time to lead with your heart.

Acknowledgements

Writing *Heart-Led Leadership* has been a journey of reflection, growth, and gratitude—and it would not have been possible without the support, encouragement, and inspiration of many incredible people.

To my team at Solari Crisis & Human Services, thank you for embodying the principles of this book every day. Your commitment to compassion, purpose, and people-first leadership has been my greatest source of insight and motivation. You are the real-life proof that heart-led leadership creates powerful outcomes.

To my coaches, mentors, colleagues, and peers in the business and leadership communities—thank you for sharing your wisdom, challenging my thinking, and reminding me that leadership is a lifelong journey. Your guidance and example have shaped not only this book, but the leader I strive to be.

To my family and close friends, your unwavering belief in me has sustained me through the long hours and inevitable moments of doubt. Your love is the foundation upon which everything else is built.

To my editor and publishing team at SelfPublishing.com, thank you for your thoughtful input, editorial expertise, and dedication to bringing this message to life with clarity and impact. Your partnership has strengthened this book in every way.

And finally, to every reader—thank you for picking up this book and exploring what it means to lead with heart. Whether you are a seasoned executive, an emerging leader, or someone navigating your own leadership journey, I hope these pages affirm your purpose, challenge your perspective, and equip you to lead with more compassion, courage, and authenticity.

This book is not the end of a journey—it is a conversation, a call to action, and a shared belief that leadership at its best, begins within.

With gratitude,

Justin

To learn more about Solari, please visit: www.solari-inc.org

To make a charitable contribution, please visit www.solari-inc.org/donate

About the Author

With a background in social work and a personal journey through mental health, I have spent my career on the front lines of behavioral health, supporting individuals and families facing life's most difficult moments. These experiences have instilled in me a deep appreciation for the power of recovery, the importance of access, and the life-changing impact of compassionate care.

Over the years, I have developed a broad perspective of the crisis services industry, spanning policy, funding, and direct service. This multidimensional understanding allows me to speak to the complexities of the behavioral health system while advocating for innovative, data-driven solutions that address both immediate crises and long-term systemic challenges.

As CEO of Solari Crisis & Human Services, I lead a nationally recognized growing nonprofit that delivers crisis and human services programs across Arizona, Oklahoma, and Colorado. I am honored to work alongside a team of dedicated professionals, united by a shared commitment to empowering people in crisis and creating pathways to healing and hope.

I hold degrees in Social Work from Arizona State University, an MBA from the University of Illinois at Urbana-Champaign, and a Certificate in Nonprofit Management from Duke University. I am a Licensed Master Social Worker, a Certified Professional in Healthcare Quality, and a Fellow of the American College of Healthcare Executives. I live in Queen Creek, Arizona, with my wife, Sally, our three amazing kids—Emma, Logan, and Landon—and our three dogs: Finley, Toby, and Rosie.

Start Leading from the Heart Today

You've taken the first step by reading this book. Now take the next.

To help you bring Heart-Led Leadership to life in your daily work, I've created free downloadable resources just for readers like you. It includes:

- A free chapter to share with others
- Heart-Led Leadership self-assessment
- A disengagement cost calculator
- Daily practices to lead with clarity, courage, and compassion
- A leadership credo template to define your values
- Reflection questions for team discussions
- …and more.

These practical tools will help you apply the principles in this book to your team, your organization, and your own leadership journey.

Because leadership is more than a role. It is a responsibility. And it starts with the heart.

Visit **www.heart-ledleadership.com** to download your free resource kit today.

SCAN ME

Work With Me

If *Heart-Led Leadership* resonated with you and you are ready to take the next step in transforming your organization, team, or leadership style, I would love to partner with you.

Whether you are seeking a keynote speaker to inspire your audience, a workshop facilitator to engage your leadership team, or a strategic advisor to help you embed heart-led principles into your organizational culture, I bring a unique blend of lived experience, executive insight, and real-world application to every engagement. My goal is to help leaders at all levels create environments where people feel seen, valued, and empowered to thrive.

Through speaking engagements, leadership retreats, and consulting partnerships, I work with organizations across industries to turn heart-led leadership from a concept into a lived, daily reality. From leading through crisis to building emotionally intelligent teams to reshaping workplace culture, our work together can drive meaningful and lasting change.

To explore how we can collaborate, please visit **www.jncstrategicsolutions. com** or connect with me directly at **justin@jncstrategicsolutions.com.** Let's continue the journey, because leadership is better when it starts with heart.

www.ingramcontent.com/pod-product-compliance
Lightning Source LLC
Chambersburg PA
CBHW040919210326
41597CB00030B/5124